What a marvelous b
communicators of Go
ful life-changing lessons from the life of King David, "The
man after God's own heart." I heartily recommend it!

Paul A. Kienel, LL.D.
Founder and President Emeritus
Association of Christian Schools International

Through the life of David, Phil shows how God gives man
the freedom to choose but also allows man to bear the
consequences for the choices made. Our choices can either
please God or disappoint Him. *Crucible* will challenge how
we evaluate making decisions and encourage us to seek and
trust God for His wisdom. Because we all have choices to
make, *Crucible* is a valuable teaching for everyone—new
believers and leaders, teenagers and couples, Christians or
non-Christians.

Alejandro Colombo
Regional Director
Caminata Bíblica Honduras

I predict that when you pick up this life scenario of David,
you'll have trouble putting it down. Phil is a master Bible
teacher who will hold your attention and fire your imagina-
tion. This is "must" read!

Lauren Libby
International President
Trans World Radio

With a unique style and passion in articulating deep biblical truths, Phil Tuttle presents this all-powerful life experience in a simplified form for the believer and leader who want to grow. *Crucible* is a must-read for every leader and church.

Philip Tutu
National Director
International Christian Ministries

I know and appreciate Phil Tuttle and have been encouraged, challenged, and blessed by his teaching and the ministry of Walk Thru the Bible. The decisions we make throughout our lives certainly have a profound impact. Phil teaches us important life lessons with clarity and insight as we learn from David—a man after God's own heart.

Brian S. Simmons
President
Association of Christian Schools International

Crucible provides unique insight into the choices David made throughout his life. Some are the same choices we face today. The fallible life of David provides all leaders with realistic reference points in order to evaluate their own decisions. *Crucible* will empower you to lead with impact!

Lee Helling
WorldTeach Southern Africa

Every man or woman that God wants to use will find himself or herself at some point in the crucible. How we handle the choices can have a profound impact on our lives and also on our circle of influence and ultimately our world. Phil Tuttle's practical and insightful teaching will help God's servant walk through the crucible victoriously.

Bill Welte
President and CEO
America's Keswick

The fact that man is a free moral agent means he is created to make choices. Choices are inherent in human nature; however, our choices can make or mar us. If we make good choices, we will move in line with the divine plan. If we make poor choices, we walk in opposite direction to the divine plan. *Crucible* is practical, expository, and relevant to our daily lives. It is recommended to everyone who dares to be great in life.

Rev. Francis Olubambi
VICM-Nigeria

In *Crucible*, Phil Tuttle expounds on the moral, ethical, and spiritual dilemmas all leaders confront. Phil teaches that God may use certain scenarios to develop our character, that decisions imply a power transcending the present, and that mistakes, though hard, are enlightening. This book will help you consider God's character before making decisions while exercising your leadership.

Dr. Alejandro Oviedo
Regional Director
Caminata Bíblica Honduras

Phil Tuttle has taken the life of one of the Bible's most recognizable personalities and identified in his life issues we all face. Phil has encouraged us with reminders of David's victories and exhorted us with sobering reminders of David's failures. *Crucible* helps us learn from a man who was once a king—and in the process causes us to look at our hearts.

Walt Wiley
Winning With Encouragement Ministries

Phil Tuttle understands what it means to be in God's crucible. I highly recommend this book and the small group DVD series he has developed to help you understand your own crucible experience!

Phillip R. Walker, Ph.D.
President, International Christian Ministries

Nearly everyone can make a few good decisions in their lives. However, here's the challenge: Great spiritual leadership requires stringing together hundreds of excellent decisions. *Crucible* reveals not only why this is valuable, but also how it can be accomplished.

Kurt Parker, Senior Minister
Harborside Christian Church
Safety Harbor, Florida

I've often wondered why God chose not to prevent David from falling into sin since David was a man after God's own heart. And why was God so angry at David and answered him aggressively when he wanted to build a house for the Lord? Phil Tuttle, led by the Holy Spirit, answers those two questions and more in *Crucible*.

Wahid Wahba
Founder and President, Middle East Leadership
Training Institute (MELTI)

Crucible teaches us that David was an ordinary man who had the kind of character, faith, truth, resolve, integrity, humility, sacrifice, and expectancy that enabled him to be "a man after God's own heart." Phil reveals how David faced life's ordinary circumstances—succeeding in some while failing in others, but victoriously overcame and had a heart to reconcile to God. *Crucible* helps us learn from the examples of David's life and become as fit for God's purposes as he was.

Rev. Vallab Sathyabal
Regional Director,
WorldTeach South Asia

This book is replete with rich understanding of spiritual truths and practical wisdom. Leaders and ordinary people will walk away with a biblical foundation on which to build their worldview. Well done, Phil!

Yuri Shelestun
Regional Director
CIS Kiev Ukraine
Pastor of Good Wharf Church

CRUCIBLE

The Choices That Change Your Life Forever

CRUCIBLE

By Phil Tuttle
with Chris Tiegreen and Walk Thru the Bible

B&H
PUBLISHING GROUP
NASHVILLE, TENNESSEE

978-1-4336-8328-2

Published by B&H Publishing Group
Nashville, Tennessee

Published in association with:
Walk Thru the Bible
4201 North Peachtree Road, Atlanta, GA 30341-1207
www.walkthru.org / 1.800.361.6131

Dewey Decimal Classification: 248.84
Subject Heading: CHRISTIAN LIFE \ DAVID, KING OF ISRAEL
\ DECISION MAKING

Unless otherwise noted, all Scripture quotations are
taken from the New International Version.® Copyright
© 1973, 1978, 1984 by International Bible Society. Used by
permission of Zondervan Publishing House. Also used:
New King James Version (NKJV), copyright © 1979, 1980, 1982,
Thomas Nelson Publishers. Used by permission.

1 2 3 4 5 6 7 8 • 18 17 16 15 14

Crucible is dedicated to my father, Gail L. Tuttle.

Like David, he fought a giant as a teenager when he stepped forward to confront Hitler's Third Reich on the battlefields of France and Germany.

Like David, he based his choices on God's truth rather than on comfort or convenience.

Like David, he sometimes struggled and stumbled.

Like David, he was humble and willingly repented when he made mistakes.

Like David, he intentionally did everything he could do to prepare his son for success.

And like David, he is truly a man after God's own heart.

I love you, Dad, and respect you more than you will ever understand.

ACKNOWLEDGMENTS

It's not an overstatement to say that *Crucible* is the fulfillment of a lifelong dream. I've wanted to write this book ever since I taught my first series of messages on the life of David. His story resonated with me and helped me understand my own crucible experiences and how God changes our hearts to be more like His. I knew that what I'd discovered in His Word needed to be shared with as many people as possible.

To have a dream, yet not have the skill set or resources to share it can be very frustrating. I'm so thankful that God has graciously surrounded me with an amazing team of talented people who have given joyfully of their time, skills, and resources to bring *Crucible* to life.

Chris Tiegreen took my spoken words and transformed them into this manuscript. He has an unequaled ability to wrap profound thoughts in simple words. This book is a much more accurate reflection of our Lord's heart because of Chris's lifelong passion for God and His Word.

I am blessed to work with an incredible group of people at Walk Thru the Bible who took my original teaching and turned it into a whole family of resources including a small group DVD series, workbook, website, live event, and this book. There isn't enough room to list everything they did, but trust me when I say, "Even if I could have done it without them, I wouldn't have wanted to." Thank you, David Hodge, Donna Pennell, Genny Baxley, Fredrick Byrd, Jerry Hull, John Houchens, Kara Holland, Paul Phillips, Rich Leland, Sandie Severnak, and Tony Gibbs.

It's one thing to write for your own culture; it's entirely different to write for the world. I'm so thankful for our global leaders who helped shape the international version of this series. They have provided encouragement and honest feedback through each step of the process. *Crucible* is now in their hands as they share the lessons of David's life in more than twenty languages and one hundred countries.

I also want to thank several vendors who have become true partners and friends. Thank you to Michael Koiner, Michelle Strickland, Dave Ball and the team at Lenscape Studios, and Matt Gore and the crew at NightGlass Media Group.

No resource like this starts out in its final form. I'd be remiss not to mention the staff and congregation at my home church, The Bridge, in Lawrenceville, Georgia. Thank you for enduring the first version of these messages and pretending to enjoy it!

Even with all the people involved in this project, it would not have been possible without the generosity of Judy Huber. Thank you for your vision to share *Crucible* with the world.

As much as we'd like to avoid it, life is a series of crucible moments. My wife, Ellen, and children, Emily and Philip, have helped me understand and embrace God's work in my life. As we continue our lifelong adventure together, the three of you assure me that our crucible moments have been worth every second.

CONTENTS

INTRODUCTION

M r. Gore, the chemistry teacher, was my favorite teacher in high school. Maybe it was because of his fiendish laugh, or perhaps his habit of booby-trapping the classroom floor with a substance that would create little explosions whenever a late student walked into the room. You know—things a teacher could never get away with in a post-9/11 world. But I also liked how he expressed things that I would remember for years to come. Even today, I still remember these words: "Nothing comes out of the crucible the same as it went in."

Mr. Gore described how the crucible reveals everything. Some substances are broken down by the fire of the crucible. Others are refined. Some molecules bond there, while others are separated. Impurities rise to the surface, where they can be skimmed off the top or left to reintegrate back into the substance when the crucible cools. The crucible is a place where substances are refined and defined and changed.

As I've taught about the defining moments of King David's life—the crucible moments that revealed or shaped who he was—I've found that the term *crucible* is familiar to

1

some people but not to others. It's one of those words we don't use every day. So before we go on, I should probably be clear on what we're talking about. Here are the dictionary definitions for a crucible, straight out of Merriam-Webster's online:

1. a vessel of a very refractory material (as porcelain) used for melting and calcining a substance that requires a high degree of heat
2. a severe test
3. a place or situation in which concentrated forces interact to cause or influence change or development[1]

The first definition, the one Mr. Gore introduced me to in chemistry class, is the picture from which the other two definitions grew. The crucible, usually porcelain, is used for melting a substance in order to separate its elements or change them through intense heat. It can be used to burn off the dross in precious metals in order to purify them. Everything in the crucible is affected, and only the elements that can stand the heat remain.

Because of that refining process, the word has also come to mean "a severe test." That's certainly an appropriate description of these moments in the life of David. There were times when circumstances put intense pressure on him, and what was in his heart came to the surface. But if I had any doubts that this word was fitting for these critical moments in David's life, the third definition relieved them completely: "a place or situation in which concentrated forces interact to cause or influence change or development." That's exactly what David went through—and what all of us will go through too. Proverbs 17:3 is more than just a casual observation. It's a profound statement about God's methods: "The crucible for silver and the furnace for gold, but the LORD tests the heart." The crucible moments of our lives can reveal what's in our hearts and develop us into the people God wants us to be.

So this book is called *Crucible: The Choices That Change Your Life Forever.* Ultimately, this isn't a book about David; it's about us. It begins by exploring the question, How did God transform a young shepherd boy into the greatest king Israel ever had? It's encouraging that He did, but it was an excruciatingly long process to take this shepherd with a tender heart toward God and make him into somebody with the wisdom, discernment, boldness, and faith to lead God's people. How did that happen? How was he transformed and equipped to have a heart after God's own heart? The reason these questions are important is not because we need to understand David but because we need to understand God. This isn't just a history lesson. This is how God works in us. At any stage in our lives, He is preparing us for something.

> "The crucible for silver and the furnace for gold, but the LORD tests the heart."

I would love for it to be said of me one day that I have a heart after God's own heart. Most men and women who follow Him would love to know that about themselves too. The same could be said of us not just as individuals but as families, churches, and other organizations. The way God works with individuals can also apply to groups. How do we collectively bring pleasure to God? How do we connect with His heart in a way that develops His heart within us? The answer, whether for individuals or groups, is the same: the crucible.

Mr. Gore was right. Nothing comes out of the crucible the same as it went in. The crucible reveals everything. In the crucible moments of our lives, character will be revealed. Sometimes it will be refined and even defined. Connections and bonds will be made. Impurities will rise to the top. We can skim them off the top and be done with them, or we can squander the opportunity and let them float right back into our character. But the opportunity for growth and development is always there. When the heat is on, some things happen that would not have been possible before.

It's very likely that regardless of when you picked up this book, there's something going on in your life that could be called a crucible. Maybe it's a health crisis—for you personally or someone close to you. Maybe it's a burden for a close friend or family member who doesn't share your faith. Perhaps it's an unwanted and unexpected career transition, a financial crunch, a faltering business, or a foreclosure. It could be a marriage crisis, a rebellious child, an unreasonable boss, a legal battle, or just about anything else. It may be self-inflicted or the result of someone else's mistakes and selfishness. Or it could simply be part of living in a fallen world. There's no shortage of challenges in this world to put intense pressure on our lives. We all go through crucibles, sometimes one after another after another for years.

The question isn't whether we are going to experience the crucible. The question for each of us is how we are going to respond in the midst of it. Sometimes we ask God a lot of questions, usually beginning with the word *why*. We're often tempted to think that somewhere we got off course, and perhaps that's true on occasion. But more often, the reason—not the whole reason, but part of it—that God gives us is this: There's no other way I can produce in your life what I know you need and what you ultimately want without this crucible. It isn't a comfortable answer, but it's definitely a biblical one. Severe tests reveal who we are and shape who we are becoming.

> Severe tests reveal who we are and shape who we are becoming.

Interestingly, many military training programs around the world include a component that's designed to put pressure on recruits and create a crucible experience. The final week in the U.S. Marine Corps basic training is actually called "the Crucible." It's a week of torture. Well, maybe it's not torture—that's probably only what some recruits call it as they are going through it. But it's definitely grueling. It's a rigorous, fifty-four-hour field experience that includes food- and sleep-deprivation, forty-eight miles of marching, simulated combat experience, and twenty-nine different "problem-solving exercises," which is probably just a euphemism for crisis situations that require quick and creative thinking to get out of. There are obstacles, unexpected injuries (simulated), martial arts challenges, rushes up steep hills, and assault courses. Recruits must carry forty-five pounds of gear the entire way. And every member of the team must finish together; if one gets left behind, the whole team doesn't pass.

On the final day, recruits persevere through a forced march up a steep hill at the end of the course. But when they reach the crest of the hill, their grueling test is over. The Marine Hymn plays, they get to feast on a meal that includes previously forbidden foods, and they graduate. At that point, they are called Marines. They will never want to endure that hardship again, but they do not regret it for a moment. They are forever changed.

That's the Marine version of the crucible, and it's not far removed from what many of us go through spiritually as God prepares us to be people after His own heart. We are forever changed—*if* we submit to God's processes and respond well in the crucible moments of our lives.

Notes

1. See http://www.merriam-webster.com/dictionary/crucible, accessed 5/1/12.

CHAPTER 1

Image vs. Character— David and Samuel

1 Samuel 16

The 2002 hit movie *Catch Me If You Can* tells the true story of Frank Abagnale who, as a teenager, successfully posed as an airline pilot, a doctor, and a prosecuting attorney—all while forging checks and stealing millions of dollars. How was a guy with no training in flight school, medical school, or law school—or even any experience in those fields—able to convince the people around him that he was legitimate? He acted the part. He confidently cast himself in a certain light, creating an image that other people naturally accepted. He manipulated his appearance and fooled a lot of people.

Not everyone could pull that off, but most of us know how to cast a certain image. The human race has a strong tendency to make judgments about people based on their outward appearance. We don't always see what's inside people's hearts, and our only other option is to trust the image that's presented to us. That's how we tend to evaluate each other.

Several years ago, a well-known camera company ran an ad campaign that featured the slogan, "Image is everything." Though most of us would philosophically object to that statement, we have to admit that if image isn't everything, it's at least extremely powerful. How else can we explain why advertisers often focus on creating a mood rather than describing their product? Or why public relations firms earn big money for putting the right spin on the events of the day? Or why voters usually elect the taller, smoother, better-looking candidate?

It's true. Most of us consider "image" to be superficial and then base quite a few of our decisions on it. We often buy our clothes, decorate our houses, drive our cars, choose our words, follow our celebrities, and elect our leaders primarily because of the image we want to present or to admire. More and more—especially with social networks, blogs, and access to the public arena—people are becoming aware of their "personal brand." Whether this tendency fits our ideals or not, we are highly conscious of whatever is on the surface. The image currencies may vary from culture to culture—some countries value a certain physical attribute or an attitude, like machismo or smooth speech or a shade of skin color—but the issue is universal. We focus on what's visible.

There's nothing wrong with wanting a good image, of course, but focusing on the surface rather than the substance is misleading—especially when the surface isn't an

accurate reflection of the substance. There is a fundamental
difference between the way we
view people and the way God
views them, which is one reason
the New Testament urges us to
know people spiritually, not from
a worldly point of view (2 Cor.
5:16). If we could see as God
sees—and if we valued what He
values—we might be surprised at
the potential and the calling of the people around us.

> If we could see
> as God sees,
> we might be
> surprised at the
> potential and
> the calling of the
> people around us.

Led by an Image

Israel wanted a king. It wasn't God's plan for them—at
least not yet—but the people insisted. They petitioned Samuel
the priest to appoint one for them, not because of a conviction
about the best form of government or because God was no
longer willing to guide them but because they wanted to be
like all the other nations. But being like other nations wasn't
why God called His people out of Egypt. In fact, He called
them out for exactly the opposite reason: so they could be
separate, holy, *unlike* all the other nations. So when they petitioned for a king, God took it personally. He told Samuel that
the people were looking for a human king because they had
rejected Him (1 Sam. 8:6–9). In essence, the people rejected
God's leadership in favor of a man they could see and touch.
God equated this with forsaking Him for other gods, but He

agreed to let them have what they wanted. He gave them a king named Saul.

God helped Israel choose its king, so we can't really fault the people for choosing a tall, strong, good-looking king with no heart over a less-impressive man with greater substance and character. But God did give them a king in keeping with their desire. They had wanted a king in order to be like all the other nations, so He gave them a king on the basis of what other nations would choose. First Samuel 9:2 describes Saul as "an impressive young man without equal . . . a head taller than any of the others." He had all the qualities the Israelites valued—which, at the time, did not include a heart fully devoted to God.

It's easy to look down on that generation of Israelites for its superficial value system, but we're hardly in a place to judge. We live in one of the most superficial eras in history, when people spend far more time and money on their outward appearance than they do on their hidden virtues. And when we're choosing a business or political leader, what qualities are we looking for? Appearances and lifestyles? Or qualities like character, experience, and skills? We know the right answers to that question, but our actions don't always reflect our ideals. Sometimes we pick the smoothest talker, the best dresser, or the most charming personality rather than the purest heart and highest integrity.

This tendency to choose image over character spills over into the church too. Searches for pastors and other leaders can easily become a superficial popularity contest. It takes time to learn what's truly in a person's heart; there's no such thing as a character cardiogram to quickly measure what's inside. Many pastors have won their positions because they know how to fit into the culture or talk their way out of a conflict or network with the right people. I know of a church that hired its pastor based on the fact that he could preach a mighty fine sermon and showed a lot of potential. Later, when asked to join some other men to pray, he responded, "I don't have time to pray. I'm trying to run a multi-million-dollar operation." Somehow he had shifted into the role of CEO and forgot what ministry was actually about. That's what happens when we define success differently than God does and focus our attention on the surface rather than the heart.

This is the direction God allowed Israel to go when it chose its first king. Saul was physically impressive but spiritually weak, and his weakness eventually disqualified him from keeping his throne. God rejected him and sent Samuel in search of a new king with a heart like His own.

That sets the stage for the first crucible moment we're going to explore. It comes in the time of transition from Saul's leadership to David's. Technically the transition began even before David enters the picture. Saul disobeyed God at a couple of critical moments, revealing that his heart was not dedicated to doing God's will. God grieved for making Saul king and sent Samuel to him with a message: "You have rejected the word of the LORD, and the LORD has rejected you as king over Israel!" (1 Sam. 15:26).

That had to sting. If you've ever lamented wasted opportunities in your life or looked back and wondered, *What was I thinking?* you've had a small taste of what Saul felt. God had given him great authority and multiplied blessings—everything he needed for success. Yet Saul kept demonstrating a lack of character and making excuses every time he got caught. He was a compromiser, cutting corners with God's will in order to satisfy his own interests.

Saul pleaded with Samuel to give him another chance, but God had given him multiple chances already. Saul could have demonstrated faithfulness long before. God spelled out exactly what He was looking for in 13:14—"a man after his own heart." In God's mind, the transition had already taken place; it was a done deal. Saul would continue to reign for a number of years, but God had already shifted rightful authority to the man He would choose next.

God's Surprising Choice

In a sense, the crucible moment of 1 Samuel 16 has been going on all of David's life. David's character has been under construction for years; God has been preparing him for this moment. When God sends Samuel to secretly anoint a new king, those years of preparation come to the surface. There's much more preparation to come—David will spend years waiting for his opportunity to assume the throne. But all along, God has seen the heart inside David that no one else seems to have noticed. And when Samuel goes looking for a king, God turns the moment into a landmark statement about what He wants.

We pick up the story in chapter 16, when God tells Samuel to go to Jesse's house, where he will anoint one of Jesse's sons as the next king. God doesn't bother to tell Samuel which son it is. He often reveals only part of His plan and leaves the rest for us to discover by listening to Him and following by faith.

He did that with Abraham by telling him to go without telling him where he was going. He gives us partial revelation so we'll know which direction to walk in, but never enough revelation that we can stop being dependent on Him. So Samuel has instructions to go to Jesse's house, but which of Jesse's sons will be king remains to be seen.

Samuel arrived, saw the oldest son, and instantly thought that this must have been God's choice. "Surely the LORD's anointed stands here before the LORD" (v. 6). That's the power of a first impression, and it was huge in Samuel's culture just as it is in ours. We tell people that "you never get a second chance to make a first impression," and that the first impression is made within the first fifteen seconds. That's how much human beings rely on what we see. Samuel is a prophet and a spiritually sensitive man, but he's still a human being, and he doesn't take the time to discern the truth about Eliab. He assumes some things about the kind of man God is going to choose. Eliab has the look of a leader. He's the kind of guy people would follow. He has that aura. Samuel thinks, *That's the guy.* God says, *No, he's not.*

Then God gives us His perspective: "Do not consider his appearance or his height, for I have rejected him. The LORD does not look at the things man looks at. Man looks at the outward appearance, but the LORD looks at the heart" (1 Sam. 16:7).

God doesn't look at appearance or height but at the heart. Can you guess what that's an allusion to? Saul stood head and shoulders above all Israel. The nation had already gone that route and been disappointed. God had let them have their kind of man, and that man wasn't careful to do what

God said. What we find impressive in a person doesn't really impress God; and conversely, the things that cause us to disqualify someone in our own minds—"he doesn't seem to have leadership potential"; "she's not the sharpest tool in the box"; "he just doesn't have the right people skills"; "she's lacking the education and experience to succeed"—are the characteristics that don't seem to hinder God. In fact, He delights in taking the lowly or unexpected vessels of this world and showing His glory through them. First Corinthians 1:26 tell us what kind of people God called in that community: "Not many of you were wise by human standards; not many were influential; not many were of noble birth." Some were wise, influential, and noble by human standards; He doesn't discriminate against people with privileges. But those characteristics aren't at the top of His list. He chooses the foolish things to shame the wise, the weak to shame the strong, and so on. All He needs is a willing and available heart—a heart that is zealous for Him.

Samuel almost chooses the wrong king because he is basing his choice on the wrong qualities. God spares him from making a choice that might have been just as unworthy as Saul.

As Samuel goes through the process with six more brothers with similar results, the prophet is left wondering what went wrong. "Are these all the sons you have?" he asks Jesse.

"There is still the youngest," Jesse answers, "but he is tending the sheep" (v. 11). This confession makes for an awkward, almost humorous moment. Clearly, David isn't even on Jesse's radar as a possibility for this position. He wasn't invited to the consecration when Samuel first arrived, and he isn't even mentioned until this point. As far as the members of the family are concerned, David is irrelevant to the momentous events of the day.

At least Samuel asked if there was another. He could have assumed he has the wrong Jesse, or that he had simply misheard God's instructions, or that he hadn't been discerning enough. But he asked, and Jesse had to confess that he had left one of his sons out of the process.

God's choice of David may have been surprising to Samuel and Jesse, but it isn't unusual for God to choose an unlikely leader. Jacob had a sketchy past and some broken relationships. Joseph was enslaved and imprisoned, and hardly in a position to rise to the top of Egypt's power structure. Moses was comfortable in exile, well along in years, and reluctant to get involved. Gideon was hiding in a winepress when God chose him. The disciples Jesus chose to follow Him were hardly a "who's who" of Galilee's rising stars. And the list could go on and on. God sees the character of a leader in people we would never recognize with that potential, even when their hearts aren't fully aligned with His yet. He looks deep into the core of a seed and knows what kind of fruit it will one day produce. His choices can make us scratch our heads and say, "Are You sure?" But He knows some things we don't know. He sees the details inside.

Though God has just told Samuel that He doesn't look at the outward appearance, Scripture goes ahead and describes David's outward appearance for us. He is ruddy—perhaps meaning a reddish complexion, or at least a healthy one. Yes, he's a handsome guy, but that isn't why God has chosen him.

His appearance is not a basis for confidence. It's the heart that makes the difference, and that's what separates David from his brothers.

The text tells us "from that day on the Spirit of the LORD came upon David in power" (16:13). That may raise some eyebrows among those who know how badly he messes up later on. When he sins, he sins royally. Even this heart that was zealous for God could be tempted and corrupted with power. But when the New Testament looks back on his life with the perspective of history and in light of redemption, it calls him a man after God's own heart. It even spells out what that means: "he will do everything I want him to do" (Acts 13:22). There's a pattern of obedience in David's life. Even when he fails, his heart is always coming back toward God.

The Heart of the Matter

Why does God often choose people who are unimpressive in the eyes of society? Scripture doesn't give us a comprehensive answer to that question, but it does give us some hints and glimpses. Let's look a little deeper at Paul's comments in 1 Corinthians 1 about the kind of people God had called to be a part of that community of believers. After describing them, he offers an explanation of God's methods.

> Brothers, think of what you were when you were called. Not many of you were wise by human standards; not many were influential; not many were of noble birth. But God chose the foolish things of the

world to shame the wise; God chose the weak things of the world to shame the strong. He chose the lowly things of this world and the despised things—and the things that are not—to nullify the things that are, so that no one may boast before him. (1 Cor. 1:26–29)

God loves humility—an attribute in David that we'll explore later—and He wants His people to put full confidence in Him rather than in the world or in themselves. So He is drawn to people who will best showcase His strength and wisdom and love. He chooses to qualify the called rather than call the qualified.

This theme will appear in Paul's correspondence with the Corinthians again. In his second letter to that church, he writes, "We have this treasure in jars of clay to show that this all-surpassing power is from God and not from us" (2 Cor. 4:7). Later in the same letter, he mentions his own infirmities and how God helped him resolve the issue of why they remained: God's power, it seems, is made perfect in human weakness (2 Cor. 12:9–10). That's where He shows up in our lives. When we depend on Him, we're showcasing Him in ways that independent spirits can't.

> He chooses to qualify the called rather than call the qualified.

As we try to succeed in our culture today, it's important to remember that what most people are striving for doesn't count for much in God's eyes. And, conversely, many of the characteristics that most people neglect are very highly treasured in God's eyes. Those who have a heart to make a name for themselves will fit right in with the culture's value system. But those who have a heart after God will focus on His values above all others. They may not look like prime candidates to accomplish His greatest purposes, but they are.

If you've ever felt that you don't have the qualities others are looking for, be encouraged. The qualities God is looking for will get you exactly where He wants you to be, and they are all developed best simply by having a heart that is zealous for Him. While others are busy posturing themselves and strategizing to make their own opportunities, you can seek Him first and rest in the fact that He sees your heart. And He can open whatever door He wants to for you at any moment—when His time is right.

That's what God did for David, to everyone's surprise. At this point in his life, David was only known for being a shepherd, and he wasn't even well respected in his own family. God's opinion of him superseded all others. He became Israel's prototypical king and a picture of the Messiah to come. Psalm 78 summarizes the trajectory of David's life:

> He chose David his servant and took him from the sheep pens; from tending the sheep he brought him to be the shepherd of his people Jacob, of Israel his inheritance. And David shepherded them with integrity of heart; with skillful hands he led them. (Ps. 78:70–72)

More than anything else, David was a shepherd who led God's people with a heart of integrity and hands of skill.

Step into the Story

God works character into our lives through a long and thorough process. Just because we're chosen doesn't mean we're ready. David had the makings of a king within him when God chose him, but he wasn't ready to be king. So how did God transform a young shepherd boy into the greatest king Israel ever had? Or, more relevant to each of us, how does God transform us into people who can accomplish everything He has created us to do?

That's what we'll be looking at for the rest of this book. Remember the definition of a crucible that we looked at in the introduction? It's (1) a vessel used for melting a substance that requires a high degree of heat; (2) a severe test; and (3) a place or situation in which concentrated forces interact to cause change or development. God allows us to go through the crucible again and again, not because He enjoys our discomfort but because He is shaping us, purifying us, and transforming us into the people He designed us to be. Just as we can't change God's Word but it can certainly change us, the crucibles in our lives aren't under our command but can have a powerful impact on who we are. We can't get ourselves out of them, speed them up, or control their intensity. God is looking only for our responses to them. How we respond says a lot about who we are and who we are becoming.

> Just because we're chosen doesn't mean we're ready.

David went through a number of crucible moments that either shaped and refined his character or reflected the character that was already in him—or both. The crucible always reveals character; when the heat is on, whatever's inside of us will rise to the surface. But whether the crucible refines our character is up to us. It's possible to go through it, find out what's inside us, and then fall back into old patterns. There's no guarantee that the crucible will transform us if we don't respond faithfully and intentionally. But if we participate in God's processes for our lives, we'll come out of the crucible refined and ready to step into His plans for us. Our responses to His processes determine the extent that we walk in His purposes.

> Our responses to His processes determine the extent that we walk in His purposes.

The New Testament expresses the same dynamic in different words.

> Consider it pure joy, my brothers, whenever you face trials of many kinds, because you know that the testing of your faith develops perseverance. Perseverance must finish its work so that you may be mature and complete, not lacking anything. If any of you lacks wisdom, he should ask God, who gives generously to all without finding fault, and it will be given to him. (James 1:2–5)

For whatever reason, God has chosen to use trials to develop our character. He doesn't necessarily create the trials—human nature and a sinful world conspire to give us ample opportunity to grow—but He certainly makes the most of the trials we go through. We can choose either to resist or embrace God's process. And that's probably a more significant choice than most of us have imagined.

Are you going through a trial right now? Are you standing in the midst of a crucible moment? If so, God is building character qualities into your life that you will need in order to fulfill your purpose. At every stage of your life, He is not just working in you and through you for that moment; He is also preparing you for something more. He is developing a person of substance—someone who, regardless of your outward image, has the character of His own heart.

If you ever wanted to know what His priorities are for your life, here's your answer. Most of us spend a lot of time asking Him what He wants us to do and not nearly as much time asking who He wants us to be. We're focused on getting direction while He's focused on developing character. But our actions can't be separated from what's inside us; what we do always flows out of who we are.

> Most of us spend a lot of time asking Him what He wants us to do and not nearly as much time asking who He wants us to be.

How much effort are you putting into developing your image as opposed to cultivating your character? Are you as intentional about your love, your humility, your teachability, your integrity, and your passion for God as you are about the impression you make on others, your status,

21

and your outward accomplishments? Are you investing your thoughts, your feelings, and your energy in the attributes that mark you forever as a citizen of God's kingdom, or in the attributes that shape your image for a moment in time? Most of us don't deal with these questions consciously—they play out much more subtly beneath the surface of our lives. But they are critical questions to answer. These are the issues that shape our relationship with God and, to a large degree, determine the calling and the opportunities He gives us. When our desire is to follow Him, when we choose to embrace His processes rather than resist them, when our highest values reflect His, we have the kind of heart He chooses to build His kingdom.

↗ Questions for Discussion and Reflection ↙

• Do the definitions of *crucible* remind you of any particular times in your life? Why did those times feel like a crucible? What character traits do you think God was developing in you during those times?

• In what ways do you think society values image over character? Why do you think human beings tend to be preoccupied with image?

• Israel wanted a king in order to be like other nations. Have you ever made decisions in order to be like someone else or to "fit in"? Were you satisfied with the results? Why or why not?

• What role does image play in your decision-making process? Can you think of a time when you had to remind yourself to focus on a person's character rather than his or her appearance?

• Have you ever felt called to something that you didn't think you were qualified to do? Why is that not a problem with God? What characteristics most qualify you for God's plans for your life?

CHAPTER 2

Fear vs. Faith— David and Goliath

1 Samuel 17

The corporate headquarters of Chick-fil-A in Atlanta holds a voluntary weekly devotional service for any staff members who want to attend, and regularly I have the opportunity to speak there. After one of those events, Bubba Cathy, senior vice president and son of founder Truett Cathy, approached me with an unusual question.

"Do you like boat rides?" he asked.

I wasn't quite sure how to answer. Did he want to go fishing? Sail around the local lake some Saturday? I didn't know, but I figured it would be fun. "Sure," I told him.

"Go see my assistant Anita and tell her you're supposed to go on the boat ride with Bubba," he said. So I did as instructed.

"Oh, good!" she said enthusiastically. "You're coming with us?"

25

"Um, yeah. So . . . what is the boat ride?"

"Did he really call it a boat ride?" she laughed as she handed me a brochure with a picture of a ship with forty-two sails. It turns out that Ellen and I were being invited to speak on a seven-day marriage enrichment cruise around the ports of Italy. I went home and shared this conversation with Ellen, telling her with as straight a face as I could that we needed to pray about this opportunity.

"You're right," she said. So we closed our eyes and bowed our heads for at least two seconds before she broke the silence. "Amen. Okay, when are we leaving?" I married a smart woman.

So we went on the cruise, enjoyed it tremendously, and then stayed in Italy a few days after it was over. We visited the museum in Florence where Michelangelo's statue of David is, and though I'm not exactly Mr. Renaissance Man, I was mesmerized. We stood there over an hour. You can see the veins in his arm, but only in the arm that's hanging down. There's intensity in his eyes, even though his body is in a relaxed stance—the perfect posture for someone who knows God has the situation under control. It was an amazing experience.

What was even more amazing was the conversation I overheard while we were standing there. A couple that was on their honeymoon came up to see the statue. I had seen them earlier in Florence and recognized them, and I knew they lived not far from us in the southeastern U.S. The wife pointed to David and asked her husband, "Now who is this again?"

This was his chance to shine. Sounding every bit like a proud new husband wanting to impress his bride, he put his arm around her and began to explain the story, because obviously she didn't have the extensive knowledge he had. I thought to myself, *This could be interesting.* And it was. He explained how, in a book called the Bible, there's a fairy tale that tells how long ago an intergalactic race of superhuman beings called the Goliaths landed on earth. The primitive earthlings had no high-tech weapons, but this guy named David threw a rock at the mother ship, hit it in just the right spot, caused it to explode, and a bunch of aliens were killed. The rest got into their ships and flew away, and the humans were saved.

Undoubtedly, the bride was amazed. She looked up at him as if to say, *How do you know all this stuff?* And I left profoundly impressed by the statue of David and more than a little disturbed about the state of biblical literacy in our world today.

I tell that story for two reasons. First, if you think this chapter is about a kids' story that everyone is overly familiar with . . . well, it apparently isn't all that familiar to some people. Second, if you think this story is simply about a hero who overcame impossible odds, I think you'll be encouraged by the dynamics of this crucible moment and how David responded to them. We're going to explore it a little more deeply than many readers do. I'm not going to reveal any exciting new details of the kind I overheard from the newlyweds in Florence that day, but I do think there are some interesting angles that most people miss. The story of David and Goliath is more than an encouraging depiction of how to overcome your giants. It's a story of fear versus faith and, if we look closely, a contrast not between David and Goliath but between David and Saul.

The Real Battle

Most people who grew up going to church have heard this story. And it can be tempting for many of us to assume that if we learned a story as a child, God is done using it in our lives as adults. I don't believe that at all. If we make that assumption, we can easily get stuck at a kid-level of theology. There's so much more to the story of David and Goliath than what we learned in third-grade Sunday school. I believe we need to come back to this story and many others with a fresh set of eyes.

Remember what we said about a crucible? It's a place of purifying, a place of extreme stress or duress where elements are broken down. It's also a place where substances are transformed into something new that wouldn't have existed before the heat was turned on. In the crucible, concentrated forces interact to produce change or development in our lives. Somehow God was able to move David from being a simple shepherd boy to reigning as king—that's part of the process we're looking at in this book—and He hasn't changed methods over the centuries. Just as He transformed David through fire and intense stress, He's transforming us too—from the inside out. And in the story of David and Goliath, we see an extremely intense situation and a shepherd making the right choice against all kinds of obstacles.

The most obvious contrast in this story is between David and Goliath. One was young and inexperienced, the other battle-tested and more than fully grown. One was an Israelite, the other a Philistine. One was armed with nothing but faith, the other with the heaviest, strongest armor and weapons of the day. But the more significant contrast, the one we can read between the lines, is the contrast between David and Saul. This contrast frames the crucible moment in David's life, and that's what we want to look at in this chapter.

The contrast between Saul and David opens up this whole passage for us. Saul faced Goliath with fear, but David faced the giant with faith. Fear vs. faith isn't an uncommon theme in Scripture. When you notice the juxtaposition between fear and faith in a biblical story, you suddenly begin to notice it on page after page after page. You can track this theme through Moses' ministry, into the Promised Land, throughout the prophets, and throughout the Gospels. Jesus relentlessly built the faith of His disciples because they were going to inherit the work and needed to know how to overcome fear and walk by faith. And the fact that Christianity is spread around the world today and we're diving into God's Word is evidence that they learned the lesson well. That lesson is no less vital for us today because we'll find the battle between fear and faith rising up within us almost daily. Not only does it show up on page after page of Scripture; it also shows up in situation after situation of our lives. It's a crucible moment that has a remarkable capacity to define our direction.

Everyone has a Goliath. Probably several. They don't fight fair, they don't have mercy, and they look invincible. They can make every day seem like war. Goliaths can show up in any area of our lives—as obstacles to our life's goals, as unyielding issues in our relationships, as overwhelming debt, as unbreakable addictions or habits, as debilitating health issues, as deep disappointments, or anything else. There's no limit to the ways they manifest. The question isn't what one looks like or what we have to do to overcome it—at least not at first. The most important question is whether we are going to face a Goliath with the heart of a David or the heart of a Saul.

That's the key. As we've seen, the heart is what matters to God. And as we'll see in this chapter and throughout the rest of this book, the heart is what makes a difference in how we live, the way we fight our battles, the way we relate to others, and every other aspect of our lives. Whatever we do outwardly comes from somewhere inside. Facing a Goliath with a heart like David's makes all the difference.

> Whatever we do outwardly comes from somewhere inside.

One Day at the Front

The story opens in 1 Samuel 17 with the Philistines having gathered for war against the Israelites. A key military strategy has always been to take the high ground first, and that's how both armies have positioned themselves; the Philistines are on one hill, the Israelites on another, and a valley lies between them. The valley is "the kill zone," the place where blood will be shed. If the battle isn't going well, the army can retreat up to its hill, which is far more defensible. But until the battle begins, the valley is neutral territory, and the hilltop armies are on edge waiting for something to happen.

Every day, the Philistines' champion warrior steps into that neutral zone and issues a challenge. It's really more of a taunt, a dare designed to intimidate. This warrior is about nine feet tall—even if he had no agility, he would have a lucrative career in the NBA or the NFL today. All he would have to do is stand at the basket and dunk or stand at the line and block passes. He could make millions. In those days, he was a battlefield hero. No one would dare take him on—which is probably why he could mock them with such contempt.

Not only is Goliath a massive man; he's also covered in heavy armor and armed with an enormous spear and a javelin. The passage itemizes his equipment with ominous, heart-deflating detail. This armor and these weapons are heavy. No normal man could bear the weight of them.

Every day—twice a day for forty days, morning and evening—this mutant figure would plod out to the middle of the valley and thunder his intimidating taunt:

> "Choose a man and have him come down to me. If he is able to fight and kill me, we will become your subjects; but if I overcome him and kill him, you will become our subjects and serve us." Then the Philistine said, "This day I defy the ranks of Israel! Give me a man and let us fight each other." (1 Sam. 17:8–10)

This would be a tempting offer if Goliath were not so seemingly invincible—and if the conditions were actually going to be honored. It's much more efficient to send two guys out to battle and declare "winner take all." There's a lot less bloodshed that way; only one life will be lost. But it's unlikely that those rules of engagement would actually be followed. Whichever side lost would hardly submit as slaves to the other side without an actual battle. This one-on-one duel would be more like the coin toss of a football game. Whichever side won would go on offense first.

You've faced this situation in your life. We all have. I don't mean that you've stood across a valley from an army of Philistines and listened to their taunts, of course. I'm talking about your confrontations with that dreaded enemy that intimidates you, holds you captive to fear, even mocks you and dares you to come out to battle. And whatever that enemy is—whatever obstacle keeps you from moving forward in life—can practically paralyze you. You won't reach your potential as a citizen of God's kingdom until you've learned to recognize the real battle and carry the right attitude into it. There's one key decision that overcomes giants: letting faith defeat fear.

Identifying the Giants

Before we continue with the story and explore David's choices when he went to the front lines, first take a few minutes to identify the giants in your life. The purpose of this story, of any biblical passage, and of the ministry of Walk Thru the Bible, is not to get a good history lesson and a firm grasp of the facts. The goal is to step into the story, put yourself in the position of its characters, and learn from what they went through. For this story to have its intended impact, you'll need to know where David's dilemma and his choice intersect with your life. And to know that, you'll need to come face-to-face with your Goliaths.

When some aspect of your life—some problem, issue, person, obstacle, wound, habit, or personal flaw—steps into the forefront and says, "You can't touch me, and your God can't touch me," that's a Goliath. It can be almost anything.

It's that area that, even when you are a mature follower of Jesus, still refuses to submit to Him. It's that one person who causes you to step out of character and revert to old, dysfunctional patterns. It's that habit you've given up a thousand and one times, and it still comes back to say, "You thought I was gone, but I'm not, and I never will be." It's that hump you can't ever get over, that glass ceiling you can't ever break through, that hole you can't dig your way out of. It's that "yes, but . . ." that shows up to contradict you whenever you think you've grown, overcome, or advanced. You may have had miraculous answers to prayer in other areas, but this problem won't be persuaded to bow to your God yet. And if you listen, you hear it taunting you and reminding you of how big and invincible it is.

A man came up to me once and told me his Goliath was 4'10".

"Who might that be?" I asked.

"My mother-in-law," he said with a straight face. I laughed, but he was serious.

"I can control my tongue around every other person on planet Earth," he explained, "but when my mother-in-law comes to visit, I say things that are extremely hurtful."

"Is she coming for Thanksgiving?" I asked. It was that season of the year, and I figured she was on his mind for a reason.

"Yep, flying all the way across the country."

"How long is she staying?"

"I don't know. She always buys a one-way ticket."

I was starting to understand. "Does she look nine feet tall?"

"Absolutely. I see her coming up the escalator at the airport, and all of a sudden I'm a different person." He went on to describe what the next few days—or weeks—of his life would look like. There would be constant battles over the thermostat. She would inevitably rearrange the kitchen cabinets to be organized as they "should" be organized. She would make critical comments about how the kids are being parented. And on and on and on.

Most of us can relate to that example—not necessarily with a mother-in-law, but with someone who pushes our buttons or somehow changes the way we normally relate to people. For some of us, it's a child who doesn't respond to all the parenting techniques and fit into the behavioral patterns of every other child in the family. The things that worked with the other ones don't work at all with this one. Or maybe it's a habit that controls you, a tendency to get depressed or anxious or angry, or an addiction or an eating disorder. Perhaps it's Internet pornography, which apparently 70 percent of church-attending men are struggling with. Alcohol and various forms of gambling aren't all that uncommon either. Or maybe it's something more socially acceptable. People at church might not consider it a problem if you like to shop too much, eat too much, gossip too much, drink too much caffeine, or whatever else, but deep down you want to overcome it and you can't.

Perhaps it's a discipline you struggle to develop. One discipline I want to improve is journaling. I have quite a few journals that beautifully document my life from January 1 through January 9 or 10. Maybe you want to pray or read the Bible more regularly. My father is in his eighties, and he read through the *Daily Walk Bible* a couple of years ago for the first time. He tells me we should put on the cover, "This will get you through Leviticus." He laughs about how many times he died in the wilderness with the Israelites. Bible-reading was his Goliath. Maybe that's yours, or maybe it's something else. Unfortunately, the options are nearly limitless. Goliaths aren't very discriminating, and they can be relentless. They show up almost anywhere we don't want to see them.

What's your Goliath? Maybe something has already come to mind, but think about it for a few minutes if you need to. It will help to have that image in your mind, however unpleasant it might be, as you read on.

The Battlefront Inside

Verse 11 describes the effect a Goliath has on us. "On hearing the Philistine's words, Saul and all the Israelites were dismayed and terrified." Those two words may seem redundant, but there's a reason both of them are used. "Terrified" captures the sense of fear felt by Saul and his men, but "dismayed" takes that fear to a deeper level. It's a sense of hopelessness, when fear makes you feel like you have no options. These men are shaking in their boots. There's no way out.

That's how Saul felt, and his attitude carried over to his men. Twice a day for forty days (v. 16)—that's eighty humiliating speeches—and Saul responded by doing absolutely nothing. No attack, no strategy meetings, no looking for an opportune moment. The army was paralyzed with fear. Like we often do, they faced their Goliath with a sense of defeat, resignation, hopelessness, discouragement, powerlessness, uselessness, and probably guilt.

David, on the other hand, was energized by faith. His three oldest brothers had followed Saul to war, and their father sent David to the front lines with some supplies (1 Sam. 17:20–26). When David arrived, the army was going out to its battle positions. They are thinking about fighting, maybe even praying about it, and going so far as to position themselves for it. But they are definitely not fighting. In their hearts, they are hoping today isn't the day they might have to lose their lives. We can almost picture them scampering back up the hillside, counting the hours until they will have to go through this charade again. They are living defeated lives, probably feeling a little bit smaller with each repetition of the routine.

Goliath was intimidating because of his size, but if you recall, Saul had been chosen king because he stood head and shoulders above the rest of Israel's men. So who should have been going out to accept Goliath's challenge? There was no better candidate than Saul. This should have been his shining moment. This should have been an occasion to remind everyone why they had supported him as king. But he was cowering from this battle because it looked unwinnable. His fear was bigger than his faith. Much bigger.

So Saul had actually made arrangements to pay someone to fight this battle for him. Everyone knew that the one who accepted Goliath's challenge and won would be rewarded with lots of money, the king's daughter as his wife, and tax-exempt status for life. These were some powerful incentives. Maybe Saul's daughter was a wild card—archaeologists haven't discovered her photo, so we don't know if the men found the prospect of marriage with her to be appealing or not—but we can assume at least that status as the king's son-in-law was an attractive position. And imagine having no obligation every time tax day rolled around. No need to search for all the right forms, itemize deductions, and get all your paperwork in order. Just fill in your name and write, "I killed Goliath." That package of rewards might be worth the risk for anyone with a little confidence in his own fighting skills. It's a sweet offer. Still, it wasn't enough. Everyone was afraid.

Do you see the contrasts between Saul and David? Both men faced the same enemy but responded in opposite ways. Saul was paralyzed by fear, but David was energized by faith. Saul was concerned about his own life, but David was concerned about God's honor and the destiny of God's people. Verse 26 is the first time in this story that God is mentioned. Up to this point, it's all about the characteristics of Goliath and the attitude of Israel's army, as though those are the only factors in the equation. David comes along and reminds everyone that this is the army of the living God.

That's what Goliath does to our hearts. He marginalizes God. He draws our focus to all the circumstances that would convince us that it's no use to even try, that whatever we're meant to accomplish is futile, that our plans just won't work and our dreams and desires just aren't possible, that we can't ever defeat Goliath, even on our best day. Somehow God is removed from the picture and we feel like we're left on our own. Goliath always marginalizes God from our lives.

This is why it's vital to win the battle going on inside of us before we even think about winning it in the world around us. When you go through a crucible moment and listen to your internal dialog, don't be surprised if God isn't a big part of the conversation. It can be discouraging to talk to Him if He hasn't done things the way we wanted Him to—if the Goliaths have stood taller or remained longer than we thought they should—so sometimes we back out of the conversation altogether.

> It's vital to win the battle going on inside of us before we even think about winning it in the world around us.

We have to get to the point where we bring God back into the situation—where we realize who He is and who we are as His sons and daughters—and see the bigger picture. Saul's primary concern was that he might die if he went into battle against Goliath. David had a greater concern. I don't think he had a death wish, but he knew God would defend His people, and he was passionate about God's honor and purposes. He wasn't self-absorbed; instead, he was focused on the kingdom. That battle had already been won in his heart.

Internal Opposition

Saul's fear has been wildly contagious among the ranks. David's enthusiasm isn't. In fact, he is seen as a young upstart who thinks more of himself than he ought. And the first person to lash out at him is his own brother (1 Sam. 17:28–33). When we decide to walk by faith, we find pretty quickly that we're offensive to those who are controlled by their fears.

First, David's oldest brother—the one who would have been anointed as the next king, if Samuel's instincts and the family pecking order had been observed—serves up a cheap shot about David's "few sheep in the desert." Whether from jealousy or just general contempt, he interprets David's faith not as confidence in God but as arrogance about his own qualifications. He questions David's character and maligns his motives. He accuses David of coming only to watch the battle, kind of like accusing a racing fan of watching only for the wrecks or a hockey fan of watching only for the fights. Eliab looks down on David with contempt because David's perspective is a challenge to his own.

Eliab isn't David's only critic. Saul comes at him from a different angle and questions his abilities. "You're only a boy," he tells him. This lack of confidence in David will continue until the actual battle as Saul questions his skill, his armor, and his weapon. No one is giving David a chance, but the skepticism doesn't quench David's enthusiasm. He isn't basing his words and actions on circumstances but on who God is.

That approach is a threat to those around us. Most people have accepted their Goliaths as facts of life. Sometimes the world looks at people whose fear has won out over faith and calls them "wise," "realistic," or "sensible." Some people think the battle isn't fear versus faith but instead is actually carefulness versus recklessness. Saul and his warriors aren't looking around for someone with courage because they all seem to agree that fighting Goliath would be foolish. When David comes along with greater faith, that's exactly what they think of him. He's a fool.

Faith is a great threat to those who are controlled by fear. When the twelve spies came back from surveying the Promised Land, Joshua and Caleb's faith was an enormous annoyance to the other ten who were intimidated by the overwhelming obstacles of moving forward. Even in the church, where we're supposed to cultivate faith and live by it, we often pull people back into the mire of mediocrity when their vision gets too big. That's because faith threatens the status quo, and the status quo is comfortable. It may not be ideal; it's humiliating to live in mediocrity or to shrink back in fear forty days in a row. That may not be living, but at least it's surviving. And the risk of not surviving is very unnerving. Faith pierces the comfort zone with some very unsettling possibilities.

If you've ever stepped forward in faith, you may have noticed an increase in the number of critics around you—especially if your faith contradicts a fear that has become normalized. Don't be persuaded by the status quo. David wasn't moved by his critics, and God rewarded his faith.

At this point, David slides his résumé across the table to Saul (1 Sam. 17:34–37). He tells him, in effect, "Saul, there are some things you may not know. I've been keeping my father's sheep for years, and whenever a lion or bear comes to carry off a sheep, I've gone after it and killed it with my own hands." David has had plenty of opportunity to test his agility and his strength when his life is on the line. More than that, he has had plenty of opportunity to learn how to rely on God and to know that He is with him and defends him. David has never just let the aggressor get away with minor damage. He has stood up for what's right, even against wild animals.

David equates the giant with a wild animal. He's an "uncircumcised Philistine," an outsider who has no knowledge of God's ways. And he is unwittingly defying the armies not of Saul but of the living God. Somehow, Saul gets to the point of saying, "Go, and the LORD be with you" (v. 37).

Does Saul really believe David can defeat Goliath? It's hard to know what's going on in his mind. Maybe he's just ready to get the battle going, and David is the first one to step forward to sacrifice himself to the giant. Perhaps he realizes that if David wins, the problem is solved; and if David is killed, the annoying, naïve optimist is out of the way. Either way, an irritant is removed—either Goliath or David.

Here we see another contrast between Saul and David. Saul is worried about the future and very uncertain about God's faithfulness to him—mainly because he has been unfaithful to God. David, on the other hand, talks a lot about God's faithfulness in the past. That's an important truth to remember whenever we face a giant: God's faithfulness in the past is the basis for our faith in the present. That's why David talks about the dangerous animals he has defeated. God has a great track record.

What's sad is that God had actually prepared both Saul and David to fight Goliath. Saul's experience was more impressive than David's. He had won plenty of battles, not over lions and bears but over violent men with weapons. So what's the problem? At

> An important truth to remember whenever we face a giant: God's faithfulness in the past is the basis for our faith in the present.

that moment, Saul forgot God's faithfulness. He can't seem to remember what God has done for him—or, if he can, he doesn't see God's past works as indications of what He will do in the present. David, on the other hand, will go on to write quite a few psalms that either recall God's past works or encourage others to remember them.

If you look back over the course of your life, you'll notice some ways that God has been preparing you to fight your battles. He has given you experiences, allowed you to go through trials, and proven Himself faithful to bring you through them. David would later write that God trains our hands for battle (2 Sam. 22:35; Ps. 18:34 and 144:1). Judges 3:1–2 declares that God actually left Philistines and other enemies in the land in order to teach His people how to fight. Clearly, He is interested in making His people battle-ready, so He has been working in your life to do the same. The nature of the battle may be different today, but the need to contend for His kingdom remains. Whatever you are facing now, and whatever you will face in the future, He has faithfully been preparing you.

Once Saul agreed to let David face Goliath, he tried to set him up for success (1 Sam. 17:38–40). He dressed David up in his own battle gear and gave him his own weapons. He's thinking of Goliath in the same terms as the early part of the chapter describes him—as a warrior covered in thick armor and bearing huge weapons. David has already equated Goliath with a wild animal and called him an opponent of the living God, but Saul doesn't have a vision for any other kind of warfare than what he already knows. He is relying on conventional methods to equip David for an unconventional fight.

Have you ever felt like David in Saul's armor? I can certainly relate to that. I stepped into a position at Walk Thru the Bible that was once held by the author of a book that sold twelve million copies and by a Bible teacher who had a radio program on six hundred stations. I'm the third president, and I hadn't written any books or had any regular gigs on a media network. But when I got past the burden of feeling like I had to try to be like someone else, it was very liberating. I felt free. It's good to be a David—someone who is comfortable just being who he or she is.

You may feel like you have to wear someone else's armor, but that's not how you'll conquer your Goliaths. In your crucible moments, you can't be someone else. It isn't effective. It doesn't lead to victory. You have to be yourself. And when you are, you're free to move with God in whatever direction He leads you.

The Battle

David took Saul's armor off and went down into the valley, gathered five stones from a stream, and approached the blustering giant. And the giant, with his shield bearer in front of him, moved closer to David. Verse 42 and following describe Goliath's reaction: he seems offended that Israel's challenger is young, unseasoned, and relatively unarmed. "Am I a dog, that you come at me with sticks?" he says, accurately reflecting what David really thinks of him. He curses David and predicts that David's flesh will become food for birds and beasts. After listening to the trash-talking giant, young David lays down some spiritual smack of his own:

43

David said to the Philistine, "You come against me with sword and spear and javelin, but I come against you in the name of the LORD Almighty, the God of the armies of Israel, whom you have defied. This day the LORD will hand you over to me, and I'll strike you down and cut off your head. Today I will give the carcasses of the Philistine army to the birds of the air and the beasts of the earth, and the whole world will know that there is a God in Israel. All those gathered here will know that it is not by sword or spear that the LORD saves; for the battle is the LORD's, and he will give all of you into our hands." (1 Sam. 17:45–47)

Whenever you see "in the name of" in Scripture, it means "on the authority of." We often pray it by habit: "In Jesus' name, amen." Sometimes we forget the real meaning of that phrase, which really says that everything we just asked was based on the authority of Jesus Himself. We aren't righteous enough in ourselves to pray on our own authority, so He gave us His name—His righteousness and His authority. We are asking that the Father will hear our prayer as though it is coming out of the mouth of Jesus.

So when David says he comes out to battle in the name of the Lord Almighty, the God of the armies of Israel, he is declaring that he is fighting as a representative of the one true God. And since Goliath has just cursed David in the name of his gods, this is shaping up to be a clash of deities. Which one has more power—the one with a humongous warrior who wears dense armor and carries terrifying weapons, or the one who works through a willing and obedient heart? Two armies are about to find out.

David continues his diatribe against Goliath, making it clear that he will win this battle in God's strength, not his own. And the victory won't be over Goliath alone; it will result in a rout of the Philistines, whose carcasses will fill the valley for the birds and beasts to feast on. David knows that God isn't just interested in modest victories over the Goliaths of our lives; His victory is thorough and convincing. His power doesn't eke out a win; He is the conquering King.

For Israel's army, Goliath had marginalized God and removed Him from the equation. David puts Him right back in. After this battle, these warriors will no longer wonder about all those stories their fathers told them and ask where the God of Israel went. All observers, Israelite and Philistine, will know that God is alive and well and still working in Israel.

That illustrates another key difference between Saul and David. Saul had seen this battle as his own—his battle to win or lose, his kingdom in the balance, his army on the front line, his reward for whoever wins, his armor for the volunteer . . . it's all centered around him. David, on the other hand, sees this battle as God's. It's God who is being challenged and defied by the enemy, God who will decide the victor, and God who will be honored by the result. That's why David can move forward in faith and Saul can't. David knows God wants to fight for His own cause. And Saul has already heard the prophecy that God won't let his kingdom last. David is focused on God's battle; Saul has decided he has to look out for himself.

Do you see your battles as God's? Can you approach your Goliaths not in your own authority but in His? If so, what does the first step look like? David went to the stream to pick out his ammunition—not impressive weapons, but the right ones. Then he moved fearlessly toward the giant. What would it look like for you to take whatever modest means God has given you and move forward, trusting in His power to back you up?

> **Faith almost always requires an action step.**

Whatever that looks like, it needs to happen. Battles aren't won by waiting for them to come to you. Faith almost always requires an action step. What's yours?

Victory

You probably know the rest of the story. The Philistine moved closer, and David ran—not away from his enemy, but toward him. He reached into his pouch, took out a stone, slung it at the experienced warrior and hit him in the forehead. Goliath fell facedown, and David took the giant's own sword from him and cut off his head.

That's an encouraging result, but don't assume that your Goliath will always fall with one blow. Sometimes it takes repeated volleys. I know a man who was delivered from a cocaine addiction the same day he accepted Christ as his Savior. He had a horrible addiction, sometimes scrounging through the shag carpet of his house to find tiny bits of leftover drugs to inject. It was a horrendous environment. But he never touched drugs again after he trusted Christ. But I know other people who have been in and out of rehab multiple times, and it isn't because they had less faith than the man who was delivered immediately. It doesn't always work the same way. The important thing is to keep facing the giants with faith, no matter what the result was last time. Victory will come.

What happened next in the story is a great picture of what faith accomplishes when it perseveres past its critics and onto the battlefield. The Philistines saw that their hero was dead, and they turned around and ran. Emboldened by the sight, Israel's army advanced with a shout and pursued the Philistines across the countryside, all the way to their hometowns.

Only one Philistine died when David took up the challenge, but all of a sudden, the entire Philistine army wasn't a threat anymore. Why? Because just as fear is contagious, so is faith. In this case, they both spread immediately. Before the victory over Goliath, Saul's fear caused those around him to retreat and gave the Philistines the opportunity to grow bolder. After David won, his faith struck fear in the Philistines and caused those around him to rise up in faith. Israel's army advanced because they were filled with renewed confidence that God was on their side. If David could beat the giant, they could take up swords against the entire Philistine army. And, from the Philistines' point of view, if an unimpressive shepherd could slay their champion, what could Israel's armed warriors do? One young man's faith was a catalyst for immediate and radical change. The whole environment shifted.

47

Step into the Story

We need to realize that our faith can be the catalyst for those around us. People see our fear, and they also see our victories. Others are being encouraged or discouraged not by whether we win or lose but by how we fight and whether we have confidence in our God.

Our faith in today's battles can also lay a foundation for overcoming future giants. David's "Goliaths" of the past—the lions and bears he had fought—simply served as past experience that was helpful in the present. So our Goliaths today—the intimidating giants we face—will be tomorrow's lions and bears for us. They will be that past experience that taught and trained us, and we will be able to remember the battle skills we learned and the way God brought us through. In other words, our giants today may just be preparation for even greater victories tomorrow.

Earlier in this chapter, you identified one or more Goliaths in your life. Along the way, we've explored how you might approach them—the attitudes you can embrace, the faith you can have, the steps you can take, and the authority you can fight in. How you work all that out is between you and God, but I want to challenge you to intentionally remember this story and God's faithfulness to you. One way to do that is to carry a small stone around with you in a

> Remember that God fights for those who fight for Him. He delights in bringing victory to His people over the Goliaths in their lives.

pocket or purse to remind you that David's victory can also be yours. It isn't magic, and it won't bring you luck. It's not a rabbit's foot, it's a reminder. Whenever you reach into your pocket or purse and your fingers touch it, you will remember that God fights for those who fight for Him. He delights in bringing victory to His people over the Goliaths in their lives.

↗ Questions for Discussion and Reflection ↙

• Can you remember a Goliath in your life that forced you to choose between fear and faith? How did you respond? If you are currently facing a Goliath, what would a response of faith look like?

• Why did Israel's army listen to the taunts of Goliath day after day without doing anything about him? Why do you think many people put up with the Goliaths in their lives? Why do you think putting up with a Goliath is often considered wise or realistic?

• Why do you think one person who lives by faith can feel like a threat to those who are controlled by fear? How do people respond to bold faith? How should a person of faith respond when facing opposition?

• Have you ever felt like you were "dressing up" in someone else's "battle gear"? Why is it so important to be yourself as you walk by faith? How has God prepared you for your battles?

• From God's perspective, why do you think it's important for His children to face overwhelming obstacles or impossible odds? What response does He want from us when we face intimidating giants in our lives?

CHAPTER 3

Circumstances vs. Truth—David and Saul

1 Samuel 24, 26

Are you in the ministry?" asked the lady sitting next to me on the plane. I'm usually not very up-front about my occupation when I travel. I like to keep the conversation open for a little while before getting blown off, and I've found that saying I lead a ministry named Walk Thru the Bible can make people feel awkward pretty quickly. I don't lie about it, of course, but sometimes it helps to be a little vague. But this woman had apparently been reading my laptop screen while I was working, and since she asked directly . . . well, there was no way around it. So I answered just as directly: "Yes, I am."

"Oh, okay," she said.

She had to have brought it up for a reason, so I tried to keep the conversation going. "Why do you ask?"

"Well, I'm trying to make up my mind about the whole church thing."

I was tempted to crack a joke about how those of us who have been in professional ministry for years are doing the same, but it probably wasn't a great time for that. So I just asked her why.

She began to tell me her story. For years she had been a dedicated Christian, very involved in church. But after a bitter divorce, it took some time to reconnect with God. She had to rediscover that God is not like an ex-husband. He never breaks His promises and is faithful to His vows. As she began to realize that God had not betrayed her and that she could always count on Him, she grew more excited about her relationship with Him, got interested in digging deeper into the Bible, and started going to a new church.

Even though she was going through a renewal in her faith, she still had a lot of bitterness about her marriage. She and her ex-husband were playing tug-of-war with the children, and she wrestled with unforgiveness. With so many unresolved issues, she knew in her heart that the last thing she needed was another man in her life.

I could see where this story was headed, but I had no idea how she was going to get there. She continued to describe her new church—how the pastor and his wife took an interest in her and helped her through some hard times. Then a man who had just moved into the community—"an amazing guy," she said—started coming to the church. Pretty soon, he and the pastor were spending a lot of time together. He would take the pastor to play golf every Monday. He gave money to some projects that had been longtime needs at the church. After about three months, the church made him a deacon. A few months after that, he was elected chairman of the board. He was a mover and shaker. He knew how to get things done, and he knew how to relate to people. He fit right in.

Pretty soon, the pastor began talking to this woman, who was still recovering from her divorce and regaining ground spiritually, about the new guy. "Have you ever met a greater guy?" he would ask. "He's got an eye for you, you know," he suggested. He talked about how wonderful it was for this man to come to church and get involved right away. He pointed out the timing—how she and this amazing guy started coming to the church at about the same time. From all appearances, they were made for each other. The pastor made a pretty convincing case that this would be a great relationship for her. "All the stars have aligned to bring you two together," he said.

I felt pretty sure that the aligning of stars doesn't make for great theology, but I withheld judgment and kept listening. Then she told me how she and this man were soon engaged, and how a long engagement didn't make much sense, so they married about two months later. "We had been together a couple of years when I found out he was sexually abusing both of my children. He drained my bank account, and he hadn't even given us his real name. He's a con man, and this wasn't the first time he had pulled this scam."

Wow. What do you say to a story like that? Clearly something went wrong; God did not lead this dear woman into a catastrophic relationship simply by lining up all the circumstances for it. And while this was obviously not the time to point out the mistakes—she was well aware of them and needed encouragement and comfort—her story

> When trying to discern God's will, we often value an open door more than we value truth.

made me think about how often we assume that God is revealing His will to us through the circumstances around us, even when those circumstances aren't pointing us toward a healthy or godly decision. When trying to discern God's will, we often value an open door more than we value truth.

A Divine Setup?

Before David ever entered the picture, Saul got impatient while waiting for Samuel the priest to show up and make an offering to God, so he defied divine instructions and made the offering himself. When Samuel got there, he had some harsh prophetic words for the king. God would have established Saul's reign if Saul had shown he could keep God's commands, but now God was looking instead for "a man after his own heart" to replace Saul as king (1 Sam. 13:14).

How sobering. Those are some serious consequences. The "opportunity costs" don't get much bigger than that. Saul lost everything because of a rash decision to fudge on God's instructions. He later begged Samuel for a different prophetic word, desperately grabbing hold of Samuel's cloak as if it were the only remnant of his own kingship. But Samuel assured Saul that God isn't swayed like humans are. We may wonder why God put Saul in leadership to begin with, knowing how fickle his heart was, but there's clearly an illustration for us in his rise and fall. The guy who looked like a great leader didn't have the character for it. And God took the opportunity to explain exactly what kind of person He was looking for: "a man after his own heart."

Saul was told again in chapter 15 that he would be replaced. Then in chapter 16—a passage we looked at earlier—Samuel would anoint David as the future king. All of that happened before David slew Goliath. David was promoted and honored in Saul's court for a time after his victory over the giant, but he did not remain in the king's favor for long. Saul, in keeping with his pattern of fear, saw David as a threat. He tried to get rid of David indirectly by sending him out to battle against the Philistines and later by demanding a dangerous "bride price" to marry one of his daughters. But David succeeded in everything because God was with him. The two men ended up in bitter conflict for years, with Saul pursuing David with rabid jealousy.

So, from all appearances, the situation contradicted God's stated purposes. Saul was still king. God had said Saul was on his way out and David was on his way in. One man had received God's judgment; the other had received His blessing. But the circumstances didn't yet reflect a change. And there comes a time during David's long wait when just a little bit of human action can turn the situation around and help it line up with God's plan. A door opens up beautifully for David to make a critical choice. It looks like a divine setup.

David's Golden Opportunity

David has an opportunity to kill Saul, end his own exile, and assume the throne of Israel. For us to really understand the significance of his choices, we have to put ourselves in his shoes.

Imagine for a moment that you've been designated by God as the next king. The nation's spiritual leader has said so, very clearly on instructions from God Himself. It probably sounded like an imminent transition when Samuel anointed you and blessed you as the next king, but no one actually said when it would happen. For a little while, it looked as if circumstances were heading in that direction. But then everything took a turn for the worse. The current king wasn't deposed, and he didn't die. He's still very much alive—and very angry that you're more popular than him. He's a desperate man, and he spends years—not months, but years—trying to kill you. In order to escape his reach, you have to hide out in barren deserts, go undercover in enemy territory (and pretend you're insane so the enemy won't try to kill you too), never stay in one place for too long, and prepare yourself for an attack that could happen at any moment. That's a pretty stressful way to live. You have some loyal warriors who have chosen to follow you, but your rogue little army is no match for the king's vast resources. You rely on your wits and your God. You have to. The only other option is surrender and death.

This is one of the reasons David wrote so many psalms about being surrounded by enemies on every side and how faith in God allows him to sleep in safety. He knew what it was like to live on the edge of his seat for years. And he had plenty of opportunity to question God's plan. Was Samuel wrong about him being the next king? Had David done something wrong to cause God to change His mind? After all, God had rescinded His assignment for Saul; had He done the same for David? Or had God truly spoken, but the king's forces were somehow able to defy the will of the living God? These were training years for David, during which he had ample time to wrestle with questions like these, learn the ways of God, and build up faith, endurance, and patience.

With that as the background, it's easy to understand why David might have seen the events of chapters 24 and 26 as a God-given opportunity. Saul found out that David was hiding in En Gedi, a desert oasis near the Dead Sea. So the king took three thousand of Israel's best soldiers with him on a manhunt intended to eliminate this threat to his throne. Somewhere along the way, he went into a cave to relieve himself—or, as some older translations so delicately put it, "to attend to his needs" or "to cover his feet." In other words, he needed a bathroom break. Little did he know that David and his men had been using the recesses of that same cave as a hiding place.

David faced a genuine dilemma (1 Sam. 24:3–7). Scripture doesn't emphasize the depths of this dilemma or tell us everything that went through David's mind. It simply says that David's men saw this as a God-given opportunity, while David saw it as a temptation to be resisted. But think about the background to this story—how David had to have been exhausted from running from Saul, all the while knowing he was called to be Israel's king—and the details we're given even in this short passage. For one thing, David's men reminded him of something God had said to him. Apparently, the Lord had spoken to David about a time when He would give David's enemy into his hands.

I don't know about you, but if God had told me "I'm going to give your enemy into your hands for you to deal with as you wish," and then my enemy walked into a perfect setup for me to get rid of him, it would be hard not to make a connection between those two facts. After all, God had made it perfectly clear that He was removing the kingdom from Saul and giving it to David. That was His stated will. I would seriously consider that this might be God's plan to make it happen. And, if so, wouldn't it be disobedient *not* to take advantage of the divine setup? If God had arranged these circumstances and I squandered them, wouldn't this be an act of negligence? All the stars had aligned, right? God had made sure of it. If an open door is a sure sign of God's will, this certainly qualified. Killing Saul would seem like the right thing to do—a fulfillment of the God-ordained plan.

That's how David's men saw it, and who could blame them? They had put their lives on the line for David. Saul wasn't just chasing David around the wilderness with an intent to kill the young rival; he was chasing all of them and would likely eliminate everyone who had been loyal to David. David's men were exiles every bit as much as David was, and they were probably very tired of running. They had spent long years away from friends and families. They were living on their wits and whatever nourishment they could scrounge up in the desert. They were looking forward to the fulfillment of God's promise to make David king. And now Saul had walked into their dark cave and put himself in a very compromising position. This was nothing compared to Goliath. The giant had come at David with enormous armor and weapons, and David still prevailed. Saul was going to the bathroom with his garments wrapped around his feet! He was completely vulnerable to whatever they wanted to do with him.

David's Dilemma

Scripture doesn't dwell on all the dynamics of this situation, but it's a genuine conundrum for David and his men. The circumstances were perfect. David had everything he needed to kill Saul:

• *He was completely justified.* It would not be a stretch to claim self-defense, and no one in Israel would have blamed him for taking advantage of the opportunity. Most would probably have welcomed David as the new king.

• *He had loyal affirmation from his men.* True, there were about three thousand soldiers outside the cave who were presumably loyal to Saul, but how would they react if they found out their leader was dead? Their enthusiasm for the battle would have probably dipped considerably. You know what they say about cutting off the head of a snake; the body won't live to fight. And David's men would have defended him with renewed vigor and enthusiasm. It was an almost-certain victory.

• *The circumstances were perfect.* There would likely never be a more opportune time to defeat Saul. There were no battlefield strategies to come up with, no defenses to pierce through, no casualties to suffer. Simply kill a man while he's doing his business and then go out and tell his men that their leader is dead.

• *He had a prophecy from God that this day would come.* Or at least that some day like this would come. Could any situation better fit the description of "I will give your enemy into your hands for you to deal with as you wish"? How could this not be a divinely ordained opportunity? God had seemingly already given His approval.

The critical choice David faced in this story is not simply about whether to kill Saul and win this battle or not. It's a choice between living by the appearances of circumstances versus living by the big picture and grounding himself in truth. You could say David chose to live by a higher principle than the open door in front of him, but even "principle" isn't an accurate enough term. We aren't called to base our lives on a set of principles; we're called to base them on the character of God. God has unlimited opportunities in front of Him, but He only chooses the ones that fit His character and fulfill His purposes. And He isn't just interested in the end goal. He is often as concerned about *how* and *why* we do things as He is about *what* we do. The process, the means, the spirit of a decision—these are just as important to Him as the outcome. David wasn't just focused on the result; he was concerned about the way it would be accomplished. Through and through, his path to the throne had to look, smell, and feel like God. And killing Saul in a cave didn't.

> We aren't called to base our lives on a set of principles; we're called to base them on the character of God.

David's Decision

David recognized that Saul was still God's king. That fact was sacred to him. He pointed it out often, both in this passage and in others related to his conflict with Saul, that Saul was "the LORD's anointed." That meant not only that Saul had been chosen by God but that he had also been set apart and equipped for the kingship by sacred and symbolic rites given by God. Yes, God had made it clear that Saul was going to lose his throne. And it's true that, at this point, David could also claim to be "the LORD's anointed" by virtue of the fact that Samuel the priest had poured oil over him by God's instructions. But David's kingship had not yet been formalized—God had not yet cleared the way—so any other claim to the throne would look like rebellion. Killing Saul would have been taking matters into his own hands, just like any other political coup. That didn't seem right.

Few people in our culture have that much respect for authority. We forget that whether we like and agree with our leaders or not, God has still ordained them in their role. Romans 13:1 is emphatic that the authorities who exist have been established by Him. We can be pretty sure that Paul, who wrote that passage, wasn't a huge fan of the emperor Nero, who had a nasty reputation for persecuting Christians. So the fact that authorities have been established by God doesn't mean our leaders are always godly. Saul certainly wasn't. Yet he had been chosen and anointed by God for that time and place.

David didn't necessarily have a very high view of Saul, but he had an extremely high view of God and His will. And he refused to usurp, circumvent, or hasten God's plan. In David's mind, the sacred, kingly anointing was given by the will of God, and it would not be appropriate to remove it by the will of a human being. David refused to interfere with what God had established. Clearly Saul didn't deserve much respect, but that wasn't the point. It had nothing to do with Saul's character and everything to do with God's will. David trusted God enough to leave the process and the timing to Him. He would not lay a finger on Saul until God Himself removed Saul from the throne. And he seemed shocked that his men would even suggest such an offensive idea. He rebuked them sharply for thinking it.

So instead of killing Saul, David crept up and secretly cut off a corner of Saul's robe. And it's revealing that David even felt guilty about that. His conscience bothered him simply for cutting a piece of the king's garment. If ever we wanted a cardiogram of a man after God's own heart, this is it. David's heart was so sensitive that he regretted even damaging the king's clothes.

David's men must have been stunned. They were probably saying, "David, God has told you not only that He would deliver the enemy into your hands, but He would do so 'for you to deal with as you wish.' So . . . why isn't it your wish to end this ordeal? If you want to waste your opportunities for your own sake, that's one thing. But you're also wasting *our* opportunity to end this threat for our sakes. We're tired. We've followed you everywhere. We've risked our lives. And you want to prolong this miserable experience? Is this just a game to you?" It must have been painful for them to watch this golden opportunity slip away.

Saul left the cave having no idea how close he had come to the end of his life. But even though David regretted cutting the robe, the remnant in his hand served as powerful proof that David could have killed Saul and chose not to. He called out to Saul and held up the piece of robe as clear evidence that he meant Saul no harm. He bluntly insisted that Saul alone was the aggressor; this was not a two-sided conflict. And he was sure God would eventually vindicate him (1 Sam. 24:8–15).

It's fascinating that David acknowledges that "the LORD delivered you into my hands" (1 Sam. 24:10), yet he did not interpret the circumstances as an opportunity for victory. They were rather an opportunity for David to demonstrate his own innocence and good intentions. Unlike many of us, he didn't assume that an open door necessarily indicates God's will, even if God is the one who opened it. God can have lots of purposes in the circumstances that surround us, and not all of them involve stepping forward into apparent opportunities. And in every situation, He wants us to reflect His nature.

The Opportunity Returns

"Opportunity only knocks once," goes the old saying, and David's men likely had been lamenting the truth of that perspective. But a couple of chapters later, the circumstances once again appear to be perfect (1 Sam. 26:7–12). Opportunity actually knocks again. David is hiding out in a different desert when Saul gets word of his location, and once again Saul gathers three thousand men to go after him. This time, David is a little more intentional in his search for Saul, although it's still clear that David's goal is not to destroy the king. He and Abishai, one of his "mighty men" and also his nephew, sneak into Saul's camp in the middle of the night and have an opportunity to kill Saul and more than a few of his sleeping guards without much risk to themselves.

Again, this perfect set of circumstances is attributed not to chance but to God Himself. But David's men already know what David would do in this situation—they've seen the proof—so Abishai doesn't even urge David to kill Saul. He knows David isn't comfortable laying a hand on God's anointed, so he removes any responsibility of guilt from David. "I'll do it for you," he insists. "Let me pin him to the ground," he asks. In case David is concerned that the king might suffer, Abishai assures him that he won't have to thrust his spear twice. One strike, quick and painless.

But that's not enough for David. The issue is that it's still wrong to harm God's anointed servant, even if that servant hasn't lived up to his calling. And whether it's by David's hand or the hand of a companion, the guilt would remain.

Then David reveals some details about his expectations. Either God will strike Saul, or Saul will die of old age, he says. That's the process by which David expects to get to the throne according to God's promise. Yes, it may involve the untimely death of the king, but God has every right to make that decision. It's in His hands, not David's. In all of his running around the desert to get away from Saul, David has apparently learned a very valuable lesson: timing is God's responsibility. When He has given a promise, it will come to pass—on His schedule.

This is a dynamic in our relationship with God that often trips us up. I often tell people that there are only two problems with my golf game: distance and direction. That's a pretty good analogy for our two biggest complaints about God's ways: His process and His timing. God's process is almost

> When He has given a promise, it will come to pass—on His schedule.

always different than we expected, and His timing is almost always slower than we expected. He doesn't seem to have the same sense of urgency we have. God had promised David he would be king, but He didn't say when. That's usually how He works; when He gives a promise, He rarely reveals the process. In fact, the process is usually designed specifically to prepare us for the fulfillment of the promise. David would not have been able to bear the weight of his destiny if he had not spent years in faith-building exercises in the wilderness. When his life was in danger and he was surrounded by enemies, he had to learn to depend on God. When he needed to make difficult decisions, he had to learn to hear God's wisdom and rely on it. When enemies attacked, he had to learn to listen to God for directions. There was a method in the seeming madness of God's delay. David developed the qualities of a king in that time.

You've heard it said that the shortest distance between two points is a straight line. That may be true in physics and geometry, but it isn't true with God. In His mind, the shortest distance between two points is a zigzag. That's because He's interested not just in getting us to point B but in preparing us for it. That may seem terribly inefficient to us—not to mention frustrating and ridiculously time-consuming—but that's how He works. Scripture gives us numerous examples: Abraham, Jacob, Joseph, Moses, quite a few prophets, Paul, and more. Psalm 105:19 tells us that the word God had given Joseph tested him until it finally came to pass. I'm sure David could relate to that experience. So can most of the rest of us. It's easy to question God's timing when you're in the middle of a long delay filled with tests of character. David passed because he focused on God's truth rather than on the circumstances at hand.

As before, David uses the evidence of his opportunity—the king's spear and the water jug he had taken from Saul's side—to prove to Saul that he meant him no harm. In fact, he turns the situation into an occasion to rebuke Saul's general for not guarding "the LORD's anointed" carefully enough (1 Sam. 26:15–20). He points out that Saul's men had failed by leaving the king unprotected, and he emphasizes that he is no danger to Saul's safety. He contrasts Saul's aggression with his own innocence.

Remember that David has already been anointed as Israel's next king. He is far more popular among the people than Saul is. He could easily defend himself by reminding Saul of these facts. He could rub it in Saul's face and tell him he's fighting a losing battle—the outgoing "LORD's anointed" versus the incoming "LORD's anointed." Instead, he affirms Saul as king and himself as loyal subject. He uses lofty language about Saul and humble language about himself. He makes it very clear that whatever issues Saul might have with him, they can't be blamed on David.

As he did before, Saul offers many apologetic words and admits that David is a better man than he is. This time he promises not to try to harm David again, and he actually lives up to the promise. He will later be mortally wounded on the battlefield, and when he asks his armor-bearer to finish him off and keep him from falling into enemy hands, the armor-bearer shares David's convictions about harming the Lord's anointed. Saul falls on his own sword, and David's path to the throne becomes clear.

Discerning, Waiting, and Trusting

So what's the lesson from these two stories? That whenever we have an opportunity to kill a king, we should probably resist the temptation? That's good advice, but the implications are a little bigger than that. We could draw all kinds of conclusions about how we relate to authority and maintain a submissive spirit toward the people God has put over us at work or in other social structures. And while David's attitude toward his king—how he saw the king not simply as a person but as a reflection of God's will—is a great example for us, the implications are even bigger than that.

These two stories from David's life raise some pretty relevant issues for how we discern God's purposes. If there has ever been a culture that is driven by circumstances rather than by God's truth, we're in it. We aren't unique in that; world history is full of cultures that were not based on eternal truth. But our generation in particular is reluctant to seek God's direction, or the guidance of any deity, for that matter. Human wisdom is much more natural to us and, on the surface, seemingly more credible. We weigh pros and cons, figure out which options seem to be most advantageous for us in light of the circumstances, and then follow our instincts and make judgments about what seems best. And very often, the key variable in that process is which doors are open to us.

Many people operate under a basic assumption that an open door is equal to divine guidance, or that the path of least resistance is the path that makes the most sense to pursue. But submitting to circumstances is a very subjective process. Circumstances can change frequently. God's truth, on the other hand, is objective. It's unchanging. Even when we're disoriented by the circumstances around us and the feelings within us, we can anchor ourselves in what we know to be true.

This doesn't mean that God never uses circumstances to guide us. Of course He does; He can engineer open doors easily, and He frequently invites us to walk through them. But usually His open doors are confirmation of direction He has already given, or they are backed up by confirmation from other ways of hearing Him and following His guidance. But when going through an open door would require us to violate His character, we can know that God doesn't want us to proceed.

This isn't as simple to discern as we might think. There are times in Scripture when God gave a general principle and then called someone to live as an exception to that principle. (For example, the God who hates child sacrifice told Abraham to offer his son; God forbade Israel's men from marrying the women of Canaan, but when Samson wanted to and his parents objected, the Bible tells us God was in it; and Scripture gives extremely strong warnings about prostitutes, but God told Hosea to marry one.) There are rare, specific exceptions to His general instructions, at least as far as we understand them. But there are never any examples in Scripture of God leading someone to contradict His own nature. He doesn't entice people to sin or lead them in destructive ways. He wants us to base our decisions on who He really is.

So is an open door an indication of God's will? All we can say is . . . maybe. An open door *alone* isn't enough, but it may be an opportunity to go in the direction He has called us. Or there may be a bigger principle that would keep us from going through it. And we need to remember that there are times in Scripture when God called someone in a direction that looked like a firmly closed door, but He opened it as the person followed Him. And, as in David's case, we need to recognize that when circumstances seem to be pointing us in one direction and God's eternal truth is pulling us in another, truth trumps circumstances.

Think of how that applies to the story that began this chapter. The lady had been through a horrific ordeal when her pastor set her up with a man who turned out to be an abuser and a con artist, but she could point to several critical moments when she should have listened to truth instead of looking at circumstances. She said, "I knew I had no business entering into another relationship until I had dealt with my baggage." Along came a knight in shining armor riding on a white horse, and she set aside what she knew to be true. The pastor of the church certainly made mistakes too. He jumped into an instant friendship with a man who moved into the church, blinded by the gifts and privileges that the man's money was providing him. I can tell you from experience that most pastors don't get to enjoy the country club life very often, and all of a sudden this pastor's greens fees were taken care of every Monday. There's nothing wrong with that, but it doesn't mean the man with money should be given a position of leadership right away. God clearly says not to lay your hands on anyone too quickly. You need time to observe a person's life.

I asked the woman if anyone along the way saw through this man. She said her father told her again and again that he didn't trust him. But she didn't listen. She was an adult who was used to making her own decisions, so she pushed his counsel away.

We encounter this tension between truth and circumstances again and again in many areas of our lives. At times, I've had opportunities to manipulate circumstances to fit my sense of calling. You probably have too. When we strongly believe God has given us direction for our lives, it can be very tempting to try to work out that direction ourselves. We have subtle ways of maneuvering—perhaps a chance to discredit the reputation of people in our way or to force doors open at the expense of our relationships. Most of us know how to jockey for position and play certain ladder-climbing games, and we can even justify our efforts as attempts to pursue God's will for our lives. But when we find ourselves stepping out of God's character in order to step into His will, we aren't trusting His timing and His sovereignty. Yes, sometimes He will direct us to take action steps, but they will always be consistent with His nature. And when we live with trust and refuse to manipulate circumstances, we eventually arrive at the destination without any guilt or regret about how we got there.

When you have a big decision to make, be very careful about what the winds of culture are saying. Maybe the circumstances seem to be pointing in one direction, and everyone around you expects you to follow them. Perhaps the stars all line up. That really could be an indication of God's will because He can arrange circumstances however He wants to. But He is not the only one who can orchestrate circumstances. So can the enemy, the counterfeiter who takes what God does and twists it for his own purposes. How can you tell the difference between circumstances God has arranged to guide you and circumstances that have been set up to lure you down the wrong path? You need something more objective and more lasting than your own view of the circumstances. You need timeless truth—the truth that is found in God's Word and in His own nature.

> When you have a big decision to make, be very careful about what the winds of culture are saying.

Living Without Regret

I learned this lesson the hard way a few years ago when I was really into the stock market. It happened to be a good time to get into the market because everything was going up. Even a primate could pick a portfolio and make a lot of money. I would pick a stock based on whether I liked its letters, whether I knew what the letters meant or not. I met an options trader online who taught me how to trade options. For those of us who are in ministry, this is about as close to Las Vegas as most of us will get, and I got pretty hooked on it. I took our modest portfolio and doubled it every year for about five years. We used the profit to send our kids to an excellent Christian school. It was great.

I guess I needed someone to explain to me that the market can go down as well as up. That just seemed so unlikely at the time because I had only seen it go up. So when the guy who had been coaching me sent out an e-mail explaining that he was starting a hedge fund—and that he was pretty sure he could double our money every quarter—well, I felt like I just *had* to take advantage of this limited-time opportunity.

You can guess what happened. I ended up losing that investment we couldn't afford to lose. So did all the family members I had talked into investing. I had always heard that if something sounds too good to be true, it probably is. But now I'm willing to say that if it sounds too good to be true, it *always* is.

The Bible has a lot to say about quick gains. I violated so many scriptural principles that I already knew. Why? Because I was focused on circumstances and interpreting them as God's opportunity rather than focusing on His truth and receiving it as His direction. Deep in my heart, I knew it wasn't wise. But what if this was that one situation that deviated from the norm? All the stars had aligned, and I took my eyes off the truth.

I preached about this at our church not long ago, and afterward a man approached me and said, "I'm so glad you put into words what's on my heart." I asked him what he meant, and he explained that he had recently made a decision that everyone thought was crazy. He passed up a promotion that would have given him a 50 percent increase in income. It was work he would have enjoyed, and the benefits were hard to beat. But it also involved an 80 percent increase in travel.

"I just couldn't say yes to that and be the kind of dad I wanted to be. Everyone I've talked to has told me that in this recession, I'm out of my mind to turn it down. But there was a greater truth that overrode the circumstances. I didn't know how to put that into words until now."

I think my own father could tell a similar story of how he chose truth over circumstances, even though he wasn't a believer when the story began. I was in third grade when my dad announced that he and Mom would probably be splitting up. I knew they weren't getting along. I'd fall asleep listening to the Cardinals games on the radio next to my head because I didn't want to hear them arguing. But Dad could never bring himself to leave. I know he was probably concerned about his career; divorce was much less common then, and it probably wouldn't have been good for business. But he also knew that a boy needs his dad, and he decided to hang around until I was eighteen. Over time, God found a way into his heart, and when I was in seminary years later, he called one night and surprised me with the news that he was getting baptized the next Sunday. It was especially surprising because in his church background, adults didn't normally get baptized. He just wasn't into that. Now he had given his whole heart to Christ and wanted to express that by being baptized.

Mom died a few years ago. Dad wasn't just hanging around for me to turn eighteen anymore. I preached her funeral, and one of the ladies who cared for her came up to me afterward and said that if she ever became a Christian, it would be because of watching my dad love my mom. He had been her full-time caregiver until the day she died. This woman told me that Dad would warm Mom's slippers with the hairdryer before putting them on her feet. They never became perfectly compatible—Mom had her frustrations with him too—but Dad made a choice to put truth above circumstances, even when he had other options. And he hasn't regretted it.

That's what happens when we base our decisions on truth. We end up with few, if any, regrets. When David was finally anointed king publicly, his heart was guiltless and his hands were clean. All the tribes of Israel came to Hebron and gave David their support—not because he had forced his way into authority but because he had patiently let God put him there at the right time in the right way.

Step into the Story

What circumstances are you facing right now that may or may not be a reflection of truth? Are you dealing with relationship issues, financial decisions, career choices, or anything else that pits open doors against what you know to be true? God may be arranging the circumstances of your life to confirm His Word and point you in the right direction, but sometimes circumstances will pull you in a direction that contradicts His Word. When there's dissonance between the two, it's always the right choice to stand on truth—to cling to

His Word and reflect His nature. It doesn't matter how wide the doors are open if entering them violates a deeper truth.

What would you do, for example, if you were offered your dream job but just signed a two-year contract for your current position a month ago? Would you be able to keep your word and trust God for the future? Or would your now-or-never instincts cause you to stretch your ethical standards and break your commitment? Psalm 15:4 offers a blessing to those who keep their word "even when it hurts." But sometimes it hurts so much that we're tempted to find a way to get what we want.

Or what would you do if a slight twisting of the facts on a loan application would get you the house you've been longing for? No one would be defrauded in the lie, but it would still be a lie. Would you see the potential purchase as a God-given opportunity? Or would the need to fudge the numbers be enough to convince you it wasn't God's will or His timing? Our lives are full of ethical dilemmas like this—opportunities to either take matters into our own hands or choose to live by a deeper guiding truth. Some of these choices seem quite minor and easy to justify, but others have much larger implications. Either way, regardless of the size, the way we respond says a lot about how much or little we trust God.

When we're waiting on God to fulfill His purpose for us, the temptation to take matters into our own hands can be almost irresistible. We think we need to be the catalyst for change in our lives. That may be true at times—God does clearly and specifically lead us to act sometimes. But when we take it upon ourselves to provoke change, whether it's out of impatience or an inflated sense of control, we almost always get out of His timing and get ourselves into a lot of trouble.

It takes a lot of fortitude to live by truth instead of circumstances. Even David's most loyal followers didn't understand him. They were risking their lives for a future king who suddenly looked weak and indecisive. But in spite of being misunderstood and criticized, David knew the right thing to do and had the courage and faith to do it. It required great patience and discernment not to seize the opportunity to defeat his enemy, but he trusted God's timing and wanted to do things God's way. And because of his faithfulness to not interfere with God's process, God accomplished His purposes and brought David to the throne. David was able to reign without regret or guilt over the process.

Basing our lives on truth instead of circumstances isn't always obvious or easy, and it isn't always supported by those around us. But if we want to live without regret—if we want to look back at the end of the journey and know that we remained in God's will—we have to develop a lifestyle of truth, regardless of what we see with our eyes. Circumstances may or may not be giving us an accurate picture of God's purposes, but His character always does. If our hearts and actions are consistent with His nature, and if we fully trust His timing, we will find ourselves fully supported by Him.

↗ Questions for Discussion and Reflection ↙

• In what ways do God's promises or His calling in your life contradict the circumstances you're currently facing? Why do you think there is so often a long wait before His direction, His promises, or His answers to prayers come to pass?

• During the waiting times in your life, in what ways have you been tempted to take matters into your own hands?

• How can we discern the difference between "all the stars aligning" in a situation and God-given open doors? Which opportunities are from God, and which ones aren't?

• What does it mean to live by faith and not by sight (2 Cor. 5:7)? Have you ever passed up an opportunity because it didn't look/feel/seem like God's will? How can we be certain that God will reward our patience?

• Do you agree with the statement that "God's process is almost always different than we expected and God's timing is almost always slower than we hoped"? How have you seen this play out in your life?

• Why is it so important to do things God's way and wait for His timing? What happens when we don't? How do you think David felt when he became king and knew that God alone had arranged the circumstances?

CHAPTER 4

Despair vs. Resolve— David and the Amalekites

1 Samuel 30

I was only about twelve at the time, but I still remember the phone call. My mom answered and, after listening for a minute, turned white and handed the phone to my dad. The news was devastating. Some good family friends had just found out that their son had killed himself.

Though tragedies like this are always unexpected, this one was particularly stunning. The son was the second of four children, and none of them seemed to have any unusual emotional issues. This was a strong Christian family. There was seemingly nothing going wrong in this family's life. The son's suicide was a terrible surprise.

I remember the impact this had on my parents, and I felt the emotional weight of it too. The boy was older than me and I didn't know him very well, but I knew his sister and didn't know what to say to her. I couldn't imagine the grief this family was experiencing, and I still can't. I would expect that kind of pain to be paralyzing, and perhaps it was for a short time. But it wasn't in the long run. The mother, a great storyteller who had been active in child evangelism, became even more dedicated to that ministry. Years later when the father retired, they moved to Switzerland to run a guesthouse for missionaries. The other children grew up loving God and actively serving in their churches. They could have gotten stuck in their grief and developed bitterness toward God, but they didn't. They somehow carried on and let their grief fuel their mission in life.

That isn't easy to do. Despair can be overwhelming. But crisis events don't have to define us, and we can refuse to let them steal our joy and our relationship with God. Not long after their son's suicide, these parents remarked about how their other kids needed them. They knew they had to keep living. They didn't deny their pain or mask their feelings with platitudes. They were very real and very open. But they could make statements of resolve that didn't sound like hollow clichés. The look in their eyes insisted that they really believed what they said. They were gentle, loving people with a quiet strength that was hard to fathom. They were an example of how to get through desperate moments without getting mired in despair.

Life has a way of blindsiding us with any number of crises—a sudden death, a debilitating disease, the loss of a job or a home, a divorce . . . the possibilities are limitless. Sometimes those crises are painful but manageable. Other times, especially when they come in close succession or hit us when we're already down, they can be overwhelming, even paralyzing. Anyone who has found him- or herself in the depths of despair knows how hard it is to get out. But the world around us doesn't stop while we're grieving a loss or dealing with adversity. Somehow we have to find the strength to move on.

David faced that kind of crucible moment several times in his life and in a variety of forms. On more than one occasion, he teetered on the edge of despair, only to pull himself out of it and move on with the task at hand. For everyone who thinks life with God is a smooth and continuously blessed existence, David's experiences offer a resounding rebuttal. Life can get messy. It can be painful. And sometimes it can be hard to carry on. But carrying on is a choice that any of us can make if we know what to do with our grief, offenses, and questions.

The Despair of Sudden Disaster

Near the end of David's long exile from Saul, he had been hiding out in Philistine territory. He had gone there in a moment of doubt—he thought he would be destroyed by Saul if he remained in Israel, even though God had already promised him the kingship—and he and his six hundred men settled in Gath, the hometown of Goliath. He won the confidence of the king of Gath, who gave him and his men the nearby town of Ziklag. For more than a year, David lived there and would make raids on the surrounding territory. He would tell the king that he had raided Judean territory, but he was really attacking Israel's enemies. He left no witnesses alive, so no contradictory reports could come back to the king. From all appearances, David had switched sides. He looked like a Philistine warrior and an enemy of his own people.

As a coming conflict between Philistines and Israelites was on the verge of erupting—the battle that would soon kill King Saul and open the door for David to return home—David actually began to march with the king of Gath to go to war. But the other Philistine kings didn't trust David, so the king of Gath sent him back home to Ziklag. When he and his men returned to their home base, they found that it had been raided by Amalekites, a longtime enemy of Israel. The town had been burned, and all of the wives and children of David and his men had been taken captive. There was nothing left.

> So David and his men wept aloud until they had no strength left to weep. David's two wives had been captured—Ahinoam of Jezreel and Abigail, the widow of Nabal of Carmel. David was greatly distressed because the men were talking of stoning him; each one was bitter in spirit because of his sons and daughters. But David found strength in the LORD his God. (1 Sam. 30:4–6)

It isn't hard to imagine how David's men must have felt—or why their grief quickly turned to anger against David. They had been with him a long time. They had survived in deserts and caves and oases, and now they had been hiding out for more than a year in the territory of a hated enemy. They knew David had passed up opportunities to kill Saul and end this ordeal earlier. It could have all been over with just one thrust of his sword. But David was too "noble" or too naïve to take matters into his own hands, and now they were still on the run. A major battle was coming up, and it was possible that the payoff for this long nightmare might finally come. But before it could, they suffered a devastating blow. Their town was destroyed and their wives and children were carted off by ruthless enemies. All because of their loyalty to a man who, for all they knew, might or might not be Israel's next king.

David felt his own sorrow, with his two wives being among the captives. Would they be raped? Killed? Enslaved for the rest of their lives? Any caring man would tremble at the thought of what might happen to them. And on top of this personal grief, he was feeling the wrath of his most loyal friends. They were so angry they were talking of stoning him to death. When the text says they were "bitter in spirit," it isn't exaggerating. They were furious, fed up, and finally about to do something about it.

Think of David's options at this point. He could have sunk into a deep depression for the rest of his life, which might not have been all that long, from the looks of things. He could have wallowed in despair and decided that his dreams of kingship were just an illusion. He could have questioned God's loyalty to him after he had been so loyal to God all these years. "This is the price I pay for doing the right thing and acting with integrity?" he might have asked. It's a question few of us voice, but many of us have let it cross our minds at times. David could have gone there. He could have been paralyzed by the overwhelming weight of the situation.

The last phrase of verse 6 gives us a brief but profound glimpse into how David turned the corner and was lifted out of despair: "But David found strength in the LORD his God." We crave more details than that, but we aren't going to get them. The text is short and sweet, and it tells us hardly anything about *how* David found strength. It does tell us, however, *where* he found strength. And that's the key to this crucible moment.

Somehow, David found strength in God. We can imagine him in the throes of heartache, along with the rest of his men, too stunned to move. And we can imagine that if we were in that situation, we would be frantic and understandably obsessive about the horrors our loved ones might be going through at that moment. It's the kind of situation that prompts insensitive people to say, "You have to pull it together, you have to snap out of it," when really they have no idea how much pain you're feeling. Yet somehow David pulled it together and snapped out of it. Somehow he found strength by turning to God.

Did God give David comfort? Did He inspire David about the possibilities of a strategic response? Did He give him a promise that everything was going to be okay? We don't know because the text doesn't say. All we know is that one minute David was grief-stricken, and then after taking his tormented heart into God's presence, he was ready for action. He didn't let despair get the best of him. He maintained his resolve.

David got up, asked the priest for the ephod (the priestly breastplate), and asked the Lord whether he should pursue the raiders. God told him yes and assured him that he would succeed. David was ready for action.

It's vital to understand the sequence here. Many times we are waiting for that word from God, that clear encouragement to go forward, before we are able to overcome an overwhelming situation. That's not what David did. He found strength in the Lord, and *then* he got the encouragement and direction he needed. I believe God often waits for exactly that sequence before giving us the tangible evidence that He is with us. If David had asked the question and received the answer first, as if his attitude were dependent on God's response, David would have been finding his comfort in anticipated results rather than in his present relationship with God. God waited for David to find strength in Him, and then David's heart was prepared to listen for a plan.

The story continues, describing the details of how David and his men overtook the raiders and regained everything and everyone they had lost. Nothing was missing, and no one had been harmed. In fact, David and his warriors plundered the enemy and came back with more than they had to begin with. A crisis intended to destroy David—or at least to paralyze him in despair—turned out to be an opportunity that strengthened and blessed him. Instead of losing, he gained, all because in a critical moment, he strengthened himself in the Lord.

The Despair of Causing Pain

That wasn't the first or the last time David found himself on the brink of despair and then found his way out. This seemed to be a common experience for him. Years earlier, when his exile from Saul had just begun, David and his men found refuge in a community of priests at a place called Nob. He wasn't exactly truthful with the chief priest. Thinking he was on a mission from Saul, the priest fed him some of the sacred bread and gave him the sword of Goliath, which had been kept at the holy place since David had defeated the giant. When word of the priest's unintentional treason got back to Saul, he mercilessly had all eighty-five priests in that community slaughtered and then destroyed the town of Nob itself—women, children, and animals were put to the sword. One man, a son of the chief priest, escaped and reported the events to David.

> Then David said to Abiathar: "That day, when Doeg the Edomite was there, I knew he would be sure to tell Saul. I am responsible for the death of your father's whole family. Stay with me; don't be afraid; the man who is seeking your life is seeking mine also. You will be safe with me." (1 Sam. 22:22–23)

I don't know how you would have responded to this news, but if I found out that an entire town of priests, women, and children had been cruelly slaughtered simply because I had been there and lied to the priest about the nature of my mission, I'm pretty sure I would be second-guessing the call of God on my life. David seems to fully understand the implications of this news: "I am responsible for the death of your father's whole family," he said. And at that moment, he could have turned inward, become extremely introspective, questioned God's goodness, and decided the cost of his calling was greater than the benefit.

That's where some people go when they've been a catalyst for pain. I've heard of responsible parents who turned away just long enough for a toddler to fall into a pool and drown and who have never gotten over the guilt. I've known of competent businesspeople who made one bad decision that lost millions for their company and caused some faithful, hardworking people to lose their jobs, and they lose all confidence in themselves. Former First Lady Laura Bush wrote in her memoir that she lost her faith for years after causing a car accident that took the life of a high school friend. Most of us don't want to cause any kind of trouble for others, and certainly not a major crisis. But despite our best intentions, our mistakes sometimes impact those around us and create an enormous sense of guilt. We have a hard time getting over the weight of our own responsibility.

> We have a hard time getting over the weight of our own responsibility.

But that's not where David let his emotions go. He was a catalyst for the destruction of an entire community, but he refused to embrace despair. Instead, his very next statement expresses resolve instead. He invites the young man who reported the slaughter to join the band of refugees as they continue to flee from Saul.

The Despair of Being Offended at God

Many years later, after David was made king, his zeal for God's presence prompted him to try to bring the ark of the covenant to Jerusalem. The ark had been captured by Philistines years earlier, and when the Philistines suffered the consequences of being unholy in the presence of God, they gladly returned it. But the ark had been stored in a town near the border and put under guard there because it had proven dangerous to all its handlers. It remained there until David wanted to establish Jerusalem as the worship center of the kingdom.

On its journey to Jerusalem, the oxen pulling the ark stumbled, and a man named Uzzah reached out to stabilize it. But touching the ark had been emphatically forbidden in God's original instructions about how to move it. Uzzah died immediately, and it wasn't simply an unfortunate consequence of accidentally coming in contact with too much divine power. The text says that "the Lord's anger burned against Uzzah because of his irreverent act" (2 Sam. 6:7). God was demonstrating His zeal over His commands.

> Then David was angry because the Lord's wrath had broken out against Uzzah, and to this day that place is called Perez Uzzah. David was afraid of the Lord that day and said, "How can the ark of the Lord ever come to me?" He was not willing to take the ark of the Lord to be with him in the City of David. Instead, he took it aside to the house of Obed-edom the Gittite. (2 Sam. 6:8–10)

For three months, the ark remained at a nearby home, its travel suspended while David worked through his anger toward God. Only a later report convinced him that the ark was indeed a blessing to have around. This kind of incident is where many of us get stuck with our questions. How can a good God take the life of someone who was only trying to help? What kind of justice is that? Is that really how a loving God treats His people?

I knew a man who pointed to this story as "exhibit A" in his defense of why he didn't believe the Bible. Any God who would do something like that is not a God worth serving, he said. It was easier for him to believe in a softer, kinder God—one that stood above the misguided, angry stories of the Bible—than to believe in the God of Scripture.

It's easy to adopt that attitude, especially when God's actions (or apparent lack thereof) affect us personally. That desperate prayer that wasn't answered, that job opportunity that didn't come through, that difficult situation that simply wouldn't go away, that relationship that's a constant source of stress—situations like these can raise questions about God's goodness. "If He loves me, why doesn't He do something about this?" "If He's all-powerful, why doesn't He fix the problem?" We know God can change any situation with just a word, yet sometimes He doesn't. It's hard not to take that personally. It's hard not to be offended. And it's tempting to get mired in that place of offense.

> God can change any situation with just a word, yet sometimes He doesn't. It's hard not to take that personally.

That's where David could have gotten stuck. He could have turned into a skeptic at this point and remained offended at God for the rest of his life. After all, he had tried to be as loyal to God as possible, yet for all his dedication, he had travelled an enormously difficult path before his kingship, running for his life for years. Is that how

God treats His servants? That's an easy question to get hung up on.

As Jesus told John the Baptist, "Blessed is he who is not offended because of Me" (Luke 7:23 NKJV). We find ourselves in need of that perspective often, and so did David. Are we willing to follow a God we don't fully understand? David could have remained offended because he never really got any answers about Uzzah, as far as we can tell. The ark seemed at times to be a blessing and at times to be a curse, and he could have wavered between those two consequences of having it around. Ultimately, all that mattered to him was that it was a representation of God's presence. Any man after God's own heart would be satisfied with that.

The Despair of Being Chastened

In the aftermath of David's sin with Bathsheba—a story we'll look at later—David again had an opportunity to sink into depression. One of the consequences of his adultery and the follow-up murder to cover it up was that the son born to him and Bathsheba would die. But even though that judgment was given by God through Nathan the prophet, it didn't stop David from praying. After all, he knew God's heart—and therefore God's mercy. Perhaps He would change His mind. So David pleaded, fasted, spent long nights on his face before God, and kept vigil to intercede for his son. But just as God had foretold, the child died.

David's servants were afraid to tell him the news, thinking he might "do something desperate" (2 Sam. 12:18). And many people would have. But David didn't react that way at all.

> Then David got up from the ground. After he had washed, put on lotions and changed his clothes, he went into the house of the LORD and worshiped. Then he went to his own house, and at his request they served him food, and he ate. (2 Sam. 12:20)

Most of us don't worship the moment after we receive God's discipline. It's painful. We tend to either ignore it and stuff it or wallow in it. In fact, many of us stay in a place of regret for months or even years. Even though God does chasten us, He also forgives—usually more easily than we forgive ourselves. We may have a hard time moving on until we've punished ourselves for a while because even though correction is painful, we sense a need to feel the weight of it. We often linger in regret much longer than God wants us to.

Imagine how absurd that approach would be in the world of sports. In hockey, when a player violates the rules, he is sent to the penalty box, usually for two minutes. It's a limited punishment with a clear ending point. But when Christians go to the "penalty box," we often stay there after the two minutes are up. The buzzer goes off, the ref tells us our time is up, and our teammates skate by the box and tell us to get back on the ice. But we linger. Our motives were worse than the refs thought, perhaps, or we got away with one that the ref didn't see earlier in the game. So we penalize ourselves and let our team play shorthanded, even when they desperately need us to get back up and skate.

That would never happen in hockey, would it? There's a game to be played, a goal to pursue. Penalties happen, but they are limited. And when they're over, they're over. It's time to get back up and get into the game.

David got back up. He didn't take God's discipline lightly; just the opposite. But when it was over, it was over. He didn't wallow in it. He didn't sink into despair and constantly lament what could have been. He moved on.

David faced a related situation of accepting God's discipline but not dwelling in it in the aftermath of Absalom's rebellion. Absalom was one of David's sons, and at one point many of Jerusalem's fighting men were allied with him in an attempted coup against his father. As David is leaving the city in order to put some space between him and his son, as well as their two armies, a distant relative of King Saul named Shimei follows David and curses him. He hurls stones at David and essentially tells him that the turmoil he is experiencing is well deserved for shedding blood in Saul's household.

Abishai, one of David's men, wants to kill Shimei on the spot. No one should curse the king and get away with it, he says. But David looks past the immediate offense and wonders why this is happening. Is Shimei cursing him because God told him to? Has David offended God and is now reaping the consequences? Is Shimei right?

This moment of self-doubt seems unusual for a king, but David is a more broken and humble man since the incident with Bathsheba. God had disciplined him and forgiven him, but consequences are still playing out. After all, his kingdom seems to be in shambles, his family is splitting apart with unimaginable dysfunction, he is leaving the city because his own son wants to kill him . . . what more could go wrong? David feels enough guilt to assume that if he is being cursed, God probably put the curser up to it.

Again, this is the edge of despair, dismal introspection, and abject shame. David seems resigned to this turn of events and absorbs the insults being hurled at him. But he doesn't let himself fall over that edge. Even in this miserable experience and all that surrounds it, he still knows who God is. He still holds on to hope. "It may be that the LORD will see my distress and repay me with good" (2 Sam. 16:12). He hasn't lost sight of the goodness of God.

There are times when it's remarkably easy to slip into self-condemnation, and we can usually find a few people around us who will help us get there. Shimei tried to define David's circumstance for him—it all goes back to how David mistreated Saul, he asserts. And while his assessment isn't true—God already told David why he would experience turmoil in his household—David is solid enough in his relationship with God to be honest about his shortcomings, absorb the blows, and maintain God's goodness.

Most of us don't do that well. When something goes wrong, we question God's goodness or get really down on ourselves. We can recall all our past sins and half expect them to come back and haunt us. We know God is good theoretically, but we don't expect Him to be good *to us.* We've blown it too bad. Whatever trial we're going through, we can be pretty sure we deserve it.

> We know God is good theoretically, but we don't expect Him to be good *to us.*

This is an especially common perspective for those of us with really big regrets. That divorce, that abortion, that scandal, that time you told God you'd be a missionary and then reneged or missed the opportunity, that career you now see in retrospect that He was calling you to—all those events that make you think you were too bad, too late, too stubborn, too rebellious, too anything—can sink deep into your heart and fester there. Like David, we have ample opportunities to say, "I've failed God," and an accuser who reminds us of them often.

David may have assumed Shimei's voice was prompted by God, but that wasn't God's perspective. God still saw David as the king, the man after His own heart. He had already restored David and sworn to give him an everlasting legacy. David may have felt a sense of guilt, but God wasn't rejecting him. David seemed to blur the lines between conviction and condemnation.

How can we tell the difference between conviction and condemnation? I've heard it said that condemnation begins with your behavior and ties your identity to it, as though your actions determine who you are. Conviction, on the other hand, comes from the opposite direction. God's Spirit focuses on our identity and then points to our actions. Condemnation says, "Look at what you did. You must be a bad person." Conviction says, "Look at who you are. What you did doesn't line up with your identity. That's not the kind of person you are." Condemnation offers no hope; conviction is always hopeful. It simply aims at correcting what went wrong. God never pins our identity on our behavior. He is always conforming our behavior to our true identity.

When we hear accusations about past sins—real or imagined—that God has already covered, we have no business holding on to the guilt of them. We can expect to see God's goodness even when we're walking through our most desperate times.

The Despair of Overwhelming Grief

The last example of David's temptation to despair that we'll look at is perhaps the best known. The conflict with Absalom erupted into full-blown battle, and though David commanded his men not to harm Absalom, his general, Joab, killed him anyway. The death of Absalom brings David into a state of inexpressible grief. The text says he was shaken. He repeats his son's name again and again and wishes that he had died in his place. "O my son Absalom! O Absalom, my son, my son!" No one can console him.

When David's army hears how desperately he was weeping for his son, they can no longer celebrate their victory. Their hard-won battle becomes a source of grief. They trudge back into the city as though they had lost and were ashamed of it. They feel unappreciated. And Joab is furious.

Joab goes to David and rebukes him for humiliating his own soldiers—for behaving as though Absalom's life was the only one that mattered and as if he would gladly trade the lives of his men for the life of his son. He warns David that his men will desert him if they aren't congratulated and encouraged by the king. And David responds by getting up and moving on, even in his grief (2 Sam. 19:1–8).

Joab is hardly faultless in this situation, and his words are overly harsh. But his point was that the men who had just won a hard-fought victory were in need of their king. They almost felt guilty for laying their lives on the line and winning. All David could think about was his loss, not their gain. Lives had been saved that day. The rebellion had been thwarted. The city had been saved. This was not a time for the king to be on his face with uncontrollable weeping.

Somehow, David got past his grief and got on his feet. He didn't stop mourning for Absalom; at some level, he probably mourned his son the rest of his life. But he had responsibilities to fulfill; other people were leaning on him. He couldn't just collapse and grieve. He had to keep going.

Step into the Story

Before our two children were born, Ellen and I struggled with infertility. Those were hard years of building up hope and then being disappointed, then building up hope again and being disappointed again—a long, painful, exhausting cycle of broken dreams and expectations. It's hard to live on the edge of your seat for years.

I was the pastor of a church in Illinois at the time, and the congregation didn't know the struggle we were going through. Quite a few well-meaning people in the congregation would frequently make comments about how it was time for us to start a family. "Pastor, it's not enough to read the Song of Solomon; you have to apply it in your own life!" one wise elder advised. I assured him we were definitely not just hearers of the Word but also doers. One woman suggested we drink out of the same water fountain that the previous three pastors, all quite fertile, drank from. Finally, I explained to our leaders why those comments weren't encouraging and how desperately we had been trying. I remember telling them that I just didn't have the faith anymore to believe that our hopes would be fulfilled. And I'll never forget how they responded. They surrounded us with love and prayers and assurances that their faith would hold us up in the midst of our trial. Eventually we had a daughter and then a son. But I'm not sure how well we would have handled our disappointment without the support of godly people around us.

That's one of the primary ways we can keep from slipping into despair. We need to surround ourselves with people who know how to encourage us, pray for us, and support us. But even in our most lonely, desperate times, we can count on the Spirit of God being available to us and sustaining us. I'm not sure how He lifts us up, and we don't always notice when He does, but we can look back and see how He has carried us through. If we can avoid getting stuck in despair, He will strengthen us and help us move forward, even when we think moving forward is impossible.

Grief, sadness, guilt, and regret are normal aspects of human existence. There's nothing wrong with feeling those emotions. The Bible—including many of David's psalms—gives us plenty of examples of raw nerves being poured out to God. But there's a difference between feeling the normal feelings of grief and getting mired in despair. David had a tendency to be brutally honest in his emotions, and there were times when he could have settled into depression or despair as an ongoing condition. But he was always able to look to God and then look forward with hope. He lived within the contradiction between the circumstances he saw and the promises God had given, and he chose to let the latter define him.

That's what we have to do too. It isn't hard to notice that life in a fallen world contradicts God's best intentions for us. How well we live in that contradiction is an ongoing crucible moment for all of us. We can focus our eyes on everything that goes wrong, slowly and certainly slipping downward into a very desperate state. Or we can focus our eyes on every good gift, every promise God holds out for us, and be lifted into an attitude of hope. Some people call the former "realism," but the reality is what God has told us. We can legitimately anchor ourselves in His goodness, even when we don't have all our questions answered. It takes genuine resolve to do that—we can't overcome the hard trials passively. Sometimes we simply have to choose the attitude we're going to have. But with genuine resolve, the trials that could have destroyed us will eventually lift us higher and make us stronger.

We need to remember that time is precious. If we've embraced despair, we have to come to the realization at some point that this is not really how we want to live our lives. Like David, we can stand in the midst of an overwhelming moment and find some way to strengthen ourselves in the Lord. He allows us the privilege of casting ourselves on His strength, and He always offers us comfort, hope, and promise. When we resolve to grab hold of those gifts, He lifts us out of despair and carries us forward.

↗ Questions for Discussion and Reflection ↙

• Have you ever felt as if you needed a "time-out" from life in order to recover from a tragedy or trauma? Or even that you couldn't go on with your life? If so, how did God comfort and encourage you during that time? How were you able to move on?

• Which kind of despair or discouragement do you most naturally relate to: the despair of experiencing a sudden crisis, of bearing personal responsibility for a problem, of being offended by God's apparent actions (or inaction) toward you, of being chastened or disciplined, or of feeling overwhelming grief? Why?

• What do you think it means that David "strengthened himself in the LORD"? What prompted him to embrace resolve instead of despair?

• What role do other people play in helping us recover from despair?

• On what basis can Christians always have hope that despair is not permanent? How does that knowledge help us in the midst of a crisis?

CHAPTER 5

Deception vs. Integrity— David and Bathsheba

2 Samuel 11

Most of the people I went to high school with have a hard time believing what I do for a living. I came to know Christ at a young age, and I strongly believe that sealed my eternal destiny, but that decision wasn't very apparent when I got to high school. I had two distinct groups of friends and two distinct lifestyles: church and school. I believed in the separation of church and reality.

One of my best friends said something to me that I'll never forget. "In all the years we've known each other, I really believe you've lied to me more times than you've told me the truth," he said. "Usually after we've spent time together, I walk away discouraged rather than encouraged." This guy wasn't exactly a spiritual giant; in fact, he wasn't any better than I was. So it would have been easy to discount what he said. But something in his words rang true.

I made a commitment then to memorize all the verses in Proverbs that deal with the tongue. I haven't fulfilled that vow yet; I had no idea how many verses there were on that subject. But God used that moment. I wanted to be a truth-teller and to use my words to encourage others. I didn't want to live a life of deception but rather one of integrity. That set me on a path I've never regretted.

There are still times in my life when my natural bent is to take the path of least resistance. I have to intentionally resist the impulse to make excuses or play the blame game. That isn't great for our marriage or our kids. But I suspect that this is a struggle for everyone. Human nature tends to follow its own ways and then try to cover them up when those ways aren't acceptable. Sometimes that's a subtle process, and sometimes it gets pretty blatant. And it can take us far away from the life God wants for us.

That's what happened with David. Many people approach the story of David and Bathsheba as a warning against extra-marital sex, and if they aren't in the middle of an affair or struggling with their sexual purity, they aren't sure it has any relevance for them. Though this story certainly does have a lot to say about sexual purity, its lessons are a lot broader than that. At its core, it's really a story about deception versus integrity. And that's a battlefield for all of us.

Up to this point, our focus on the choices David made has emphasized the positive. He has been chosen for his character, won battles by his faith, based his life on truth, and overcome desperate moments. Later, we'll see him embrace humility, sacrifice, and hope. Even in this story, we'll see evidence of one of David's greatest strengths: his passion. But our greatest strengths can become our greatest weaknesses when they are channeled in the wrong direction, and that's what David allows to happen. His passion, usually applied toward God's will, is this time misapplied toward his own momentary, illicit desire. And the consequences are tragic.

> Our greatest strengths can become our greatest weaknesses when they are channeled in the wrong direction.

This episode in David's life is definitely not his finest moment. It's a choice that changed his life forever. And not only does he make one bad choice, he compounds it with a series of poor decisions that dig him into a deeper hole and shatter the lives of people around him. Like any of us who have taken wrong turns, David gets into a cycle of image management, damage control, and covering his tracks. The story of David and Bathsheba is a sobering example of what happens when we get into a pattern of deception and a case study in how God offers to help us escape its downward spiral.

David's Worst Choice

The story begins in 2 Samuel 11 after David has been king for a while. Israel's army was across the Jordan fighting against the Ammonites in the north, but David remained in Jerusalem. He got up from his bed one evening, walked around on the roof of the palace, and noticed a beautiful woman bathing on another rooftop.

At first, David simply sees a beautiful woman and sends someone to find out more about her. Has he sinned at this point? Probably not—it wasn't unusual for a king to acquire another member for his harem if she was available. David didn't exactly need another woman in his life, so this probably isn't a very wise move. But before he knows anything about her, and without the Bible specifically telling us his thoughts as he saw her, we can only speculate about whether he was sinning in his heart.

Some people suggest Bathsheba was already guilty of sin too. After all, she was bathing out in the open—hardly a model of modesty. But even today in the Middle East, the rooftop is a place to bathe, and there's generally an assumption of privacy. I've been in the Middle East and opened up the curtains in the morning to see all kinds of sights a few floors down from my hotel room. She can't be blamed for being unaware that she was visible to a king with an unusual vantage point from his palace. If we're going to assign blame at this point in the story, I think we have to fault David for lingering in a moment of temptation.

I don't know who said this, but it's a wise observation: "Temptations are like birds. You can't keep them from flying past your head, but you can stop them from building a nest in your hair." David was careless with that distinction, and all of us can probably point to a time when we were too. Everyone has passed that moment of "Wow, she's really beautiful," or "Oh, he's such a nice guy," and started down the path of inventing possibilities. We may have no intention of fulfilling those possibilities, but we need to remember this consistent principle of human behavior: Before we do the unthinkable, we think the undoable. If these fantasies aren't going to happen anyway, what's the harm in thinking about them? That's the lie we believe. We play around with scenarios in our minds and, if we aren't careful, find ourselves eventually walking them out—even though we never intended to in the first place. David got very careless with his thoughts.

> Before we do the unthinkable, we think the undoable.

Where carelessness ends and sin begins in this story seems to be the moment when David finds out that Bathsheba is married to one of his men and still sends messengers to get her. That should have been the end of the story. She doesn't belong to David, she's married to someone else. She's taken. He made sure she had purified herself after her monthly cycle, because apparently it's important to fulfill a minor ceremonial law while blowing one of the Ten Commandments, isn't it? That's just a sign of the level of hypocrisy David is sinking to—being careful about the details while missing the big picture. Jesus called this straining out a gnat and swallowing a camel. David loses all perspective. And in the heat of the moment, he makes a conscious choice to commit adultery. He intrudes into the marriage of a friend, violates Bathsheba's sexual purity, and serves his own self-interest.

Afterward, Bathsheba goes back home. As far as she and David are concerned, this is over. It was a one-night stand. But that plan is interrupted by a major complication: Bathsheba is pregnant.

We don't know what David was thinking in the time between his night of passion with Bathsheba and the moment he finds out she's pregnant. Maybe his conscience was already bothering him. Perhaps he was kicking himself for being foolish and had resolved never to do it again. Or maybe it still hadn't dawned on him that he had sinned greatly against God and others. We don't know. But as soon as he finds out the practical consequences of his sin, he shifts into damage-control mode. What happens next only makes his original sin worse.

The Cover-Up: Phase 1

David enters a frantic season of minimizing the consequences of his sin. I call it "David's desperate cover-up," and it comes in three phases. The first and second phases don't work very well, so David resorts to drastic measures in phase three. Every step of the way, as he tries to dig his way out from under his problems, the problems only get worse.

Phase one begins when David sends a message to his general at the battlefront to send Uriah, Bathsheba's husband, back home. Uriah has to be wondering why he has been recalled at a time when his comrades at the front need him. Was he being placed on leave because the king thought he deserved a break? Was he needed in Jerusalem for a specific assignment? Was he—one of David's mighty men and not an expendable, low-ranking foot soldier—simply supposed to give a status report from the front? No explanation is given;

Uriah simply returns home, gives an update from the war, gets instructions to go to his house, and receives a gift from David.

I would suggest that when David tells Uriah in verse 8 to "go down to your house and wash your feet," he isn't just encouraging him to clean between his toes. That's a polite way of saying, "go home, relax, and enjoy intimacy with your wife." That's a pretty sweet deal for a soldier who has just been plucked from the hell of the battlefield—R&R in the capital city, a gift from the king, and a night of pleasure with his wife. Uriah has to be wondering why he has been singled out for such an unexpected favor.

David's plan, of course, is for Uriah and Bathsheba to have sex so that everyone including Uriah will assume, when Bathsheba's pregnancy becomes obvious, that her husband is the father. The science of conception and delivery was much less specific then than it is now, so no one will be counting the weeks and calculating an exact due date. "About nine months" is close enough to cover David's tracks. This sordid episode will never show up on the *Jerry Springer Show*, and no court will order a paternity test. Nothing will ever come of it . . . if only Uriah sleeps with his wife like any normal, battle-weary, homesick man would do. It's a foolproof plan.

But David's plan doesn't account for the character of Uriah. Instead of going home, Uriah decides to spend the night at the entrance to the palace where the servants sleep. Why? Because the ark and Israel's armies are staying in tents at the battlefront. It wouldn't be right for a soldier to go home and enjoy a meal and an evening with his wife (2 Sam. 11:10–11). Now there are witnesses to the fact that Uriah didn't sleep with his wife when he came home from the front. David's cover-up isn't covering anything very well yet.

Uriah is a Hittite—not even a native Israelite; he's a foreigner. Some would even classify him as a mercenary, a member of a conquered people who enlisted in the conqueror's army. He has been one of David's "mighty men" throughout the years—one of the valiant warriors who sided with David during his long exile from Saul. He has proven his loyalty to the king. But he still isn't "one of us" in the eyes of some Israelites.

Yet this Hittite behaves more nobly than the man after God's own heart has behaved recently. He cannot bring himself to enjoy privileges that his companions can't enjoy too, or to rest easy while the ark of God is being housed in a tent during a time of war. It wouldn't be right to be pampered at a time like this. So Uriah disciplines himself out of loyalty to his fellow soldiers, his leaders, his country, and his God.

My father fought in World War II, and after landing in France and fighting through the countryside into Germany, there was one point when he got really sick and was sent to a hospital. As he tells the story, he couldn't wait to get back to his unit, even though he was scared out of his mind. He had been plucked out of the cornfields of Iowa at eighteen and placed into the insanity of the war. It wasn't an exciting adventure, it was a dreadful conflict. But with tears in his eyes even today, he says, "I just knew my buddies, my friends, the guys I fought with shoulder-to-shoulder, stood more chance of coming home safely if I was by their side than if I was lying in a hospital somewhere unable to help." That's the kind of loyalty that makes a great soldier, and that's the kind of loyalty Uriah demonstrated.

Do you see the contrast in this passage—and the irony? David, the man after God's own heart, has demanded immediate gratification for himself. He has to have his needs met *now*. He assumes Uriah will do the same, but the Hittite practices delayed gratification instead. He can wait to satisfy his needs because there are greater needs at hand. David has abused his authority and claimed what wasn't his. Uriah has proved his loyalty and won't even claim what is rightfully his. Phase one fails because Uriah has been behaving with stronger character than David has. David has to be perplexed and, we would think, a little humbled by it. But if he was, it doesn't show because David is too busy coming up with a plan B.

The Cover-Up: Phase 2

David's next plan involves getting Uriah drunk. In other words, he must now try to weaken the strong character that the Hittite has demonstrated. If Uriah lets down his guard, maybe he will compromise his overblown standards. But even intoxicated—at the king's insistence—Uriah chooses to sleep among the servants (2 Sam. 11:12–13).

Scripture doesn't mess around. It lays the blame squarely at David's feet. "David made him drunk." There's no hint that Hittites, in spite of being fierce fighters, can't hold their liquor. There's no softening of the words to imply that David invited Uriah to drink and the man just couldn't resist. No, Uriah's drunkenness could actually be even another sign of his loyalty. When the king says, "Have another drink," a servant must comply. David compromised his loyal warrior's sensibilities and then sent him home.

So where did Uriah go? Not home. He still stuck to his standards. At this moment, a drunk Hittite has more wisdom and integrity than a king with a heart like God's. That's the degree of deception David is living in, and that's the contrast that God puts in front of him to highlight the difference. The integrity and wholeness David has enjoyed—the *shalom* he has experienced in his relationship with God—is now replaced by a life of lies. He's building a house of cards, and it's going to tumble because it's being built on a foundation of deception.

This is a warning to anyone who has ever tried to cover up a sin—which I suspect is probably all of us. We can probably affirm that it hasn't worked very well. Even if it was successful, it was a painful burden. Life feels fragile when you have to walk around on a web of deceit. You have to be careful about where you step and what you say. It's draining to maintain a life like that. That's what David is wrestling with, and it's about to drive him to extremes.

The Cover-Up: Phase 3

Bringing Uriah home didn't work. Neither did getting him drunk. The next best thing David can think of is to get Uriah killed. It's a dreadful choice, but David can probably justify it as one casualty in a much bigger story. The office of king must be respected. David's reputation must be preserved. These are important national issues. One casualty, though tragic, is worth the cost for the sake of the kingdom.

It's hard to imagine the man of integrity we've seen so far getting to this point of self-deception. Even David would have had a hard time imagining it. If we were able to ask him a couple of years before this episode if he could ever foresee a scenario in which he would have one of his most loyal men killed just to hide something David had done wrong, David would have been appalled. "May it never be!" he would probably say. "May God strike me dead before I would do something like that!" We can easily picture him responding that way because he really did have a sensitive heart. We aren't reading the story of callous king and his unconscionable affairs. We're reading the story of a real human being who was chosen by God because of his character. That should be sobering to us; none of us are immune from sinking this low. We're all capable of being deceived.

David continues the cover-up by writing a letter to Joab and sending it with Uriah back to the front. The letter tells Joab to put Uriah in the heat of battle, where the fighting is the fiercest, and then withdraw from him. Leave him alone amid the enemies. Joab complies, and the plan works. Uriah the Hittite dies (2 Sam. 11:14–17).

Just think about this for a minute. David writes a royal decree, and it has to be sent to Joab. Who does he choose to deliver it? Uriah—a faithful man carrying his own death sentence. That's a huge risk on David's part. What if this Hittite is one of those braggart types? What if it crosses his mind to peek into the correspondence and see what brilliant battle strategy it contains? Sure, there's a royal seal on it, but what if it "accidentally" came apart? Uriah could try to get credit for coming up with a strategic initiative. Perhaps he could even get promoted. But Uriah has already demonstrated his character, and David at this point surely knows he can trust his soldier to faithfully deliver the message. He can count on the integrity that has already foiled David's plans to cover up his sin. He takes Uriah's integrity now and uses it against him.

Phase 3 of the cover-up is a tragic success. We call that "collateral damage"—an innocent victim of an unfortunate event. The sin that was supposed to be secret, that originally wasn't supposed to hurt anyone, has now had broader implications than expected.

That's almost always the way it works. I've counseled people who were in inappropriate relationships, and they often say something like, "You know, we're two adults. We're not hurting anyone. If we hurt ourselves, that's our choice." I don't buy that for a minute. There's almost always collateral damage, like a rock that hits the water and sends ripples out in every direction. Uriah wasn't the only one who died in this battle scene; several other faithful soldiers would not be going home to their families now. It's a devastating situation that began one night when David sent for a woman who wasn't his wife.

If you read this story carefully, you'll notice a lot of sending going on. The repetition of the words *send* and *sent* is revealing. In most cultures, and even in most companies today, the person doing the sending is usually the one who's in authority. David sends the army out to battle, he sends someone to find out about Bathsheba, he sends messengers to get her, he sends for Uriah to come home, he sends Uriah to his house, he sends Uriah back to the battlefield with a letter . . . David is definitely in charge. In his universe, he is acting as his own supreme authority because he has left God out of the picture.

If you think about it, though, David's solution hasn't completely solved his problems. Uriah's death doesn't cover up the fact that he never slept with his wife during the time in question. It has only removed the offended party from the equation. Anyone who remembers how Uriah slept outside the gate during his only trip home from the battlefront can still raise questions about Bathsheba's baby. Perhaps now that she's a widow, all of those questions are forgotten. Maybe her husband's death is traumatic enough to cause people to blur the sequence of events. At least David can hope for that. But this isn't what he wanted. It's the desperate act of a desperate king.

All's Well that Ends Well . . . Unless It Doesn't

This chapter of David's life seems to be over. Uriah dies, Bathsheba mourns, David marries her, she gives birth, and they all live happily ever after. Well, that was the plan David envisioned, but it doesn't quite work out that way.

I don't want to speculate too much about what goes on between the lines of Scripture, but if there's nothing new under the sun, there was some version of press secretaries back in David's day just as in ours. And this marriage between David and Bathsheba seems like a Rose Garden photo op if there ever was one. Can you imagine the spin his public relations team put on this? "We have a fallen hero, one of the king's most loyal men, and his wife is pregnant. Our kind-hearted king can't do this for every fallen soldier, but look at what he's willing to do at least for this one. He's willing to bring Bathsheba into the palace, marry her, and raise her child as if it were his very own!"

That's a beautiful picture that does a nice job of tying off the loose ends of this story. But beneath the surface, it isn't beautiful at all, as we see in the second half of verse 27: "The thing David had done displeased the LORD." That statement just kind of hangs there awkwardly, waiting to be developed. And it will be. God isn't going to let this go.

A Pattern and a Promise

James 1:14–15 describes a common dynamic with temptation and sin: "Each one is tempted when, by his own evil desire, he is dragged away and enticed. Then, after desire has conceived, it gives birth to sin; and sin, when it is full-grown, gives birth to death." It begins with a misplaced desire, which can lead to temptation, which can lead to sin, which results in some kind of death. The first stages of this pattern seem harmless, but they reap devastating consequences.

The story of David and Bathsheba is a stark example of this pattern of destruction. It's not an irredeemable example, as we'll see, but it's a very graphic portrayal of the way God has wired His world. When we are out of sync with His desires and His will for our lives, and then choose to act in our own self-interest, we are led down a path that we don't want to take and experience consequences we don't want to happen.

Can you relate to this pattern? Have you seen it play out in your life or in the lives of people around you? Is there something you're trying to cover up, thinking the consequences will just go away if the sin remains hidden? If so, let David's example sink in and reconsider. And remember the promise God gives us about the temptations we face.

> These things happened to them as examples and were written down as warnings for us, on whom the fulfillment of the ages has come. So, if you think you are standing firm, be careful that you don't fall! No temptation has seized you except what is common to man. And God is faithful; he will not let you be tempted beyond what you can bear. But when you are tempted, he will also provide a way out so that you can stand up under it. (1 Cor. 10:11–13)

There's always a tendency with a story like David's to think, *That's interesting, but it isn't very relevant to me. I would never do something like that.* It's one thing to believe that by the grace of God this kind of thing will never happen to you, but to assume it can't, under certain circumstances, is setting oneself up for disaster. That's the kind of pride that comes before a fall. Verse 11 specifically tells us that biblical stories are given to us as examples and as warnings, and the verses that follow warn us against thinking that we are immune to any kind of temptation. There is always the possibility of sin, and always the possibility of avoiding it. And once we've started down a destructive path, there's always a way out of it.

That means this pattern of desire-temptation-sin-death is not inevitable. It can be interrupted by the choices we make in response to God's grace. He always provides a way out—an exit we can take. The way out may not be easy, but it will be less painful than the long-term consequences of continued or compounded sin.

Let me share with you what I hear from men all the time that illustrates these truths. I hear this again and again: "Phil, I don't know what happened when God created me. I may have missed the line for brains, but I think I went through the line for hormones at least twice. I must have extra. I don't know anyone who struggles like this, but sex runs through my brain 24/7."

The amazing thing about that comment is how often I hear it. My answer is, "Yeah, you're right. You're unique, just like everyone else." Somehow Satan is able to isolate us and make us think we have a unique, deep, dark secret that no one else struggles with. And he convinces us that we'd better hide that secret from friends, family, group members, and everyone else, because if others knew, we'd lose all respect. He never tells us that when a secret gets dragged out into the light, it loses its power. So let me encourage you—whatever the sin or the secret is, whether you're male or female, whether it's a matter of sexual purity or integrity or attitudes or habits—to find someone to share it with. There are people in your life who are safe to talk to, people who won't be shocked, people who know how to keep things in confidence. Whatever your temptation is, it is common to human beings. Bringing it into the light is a great first step toward breaking its power.

Then we're given a promise. God provides a way out. Always. Imagine, for example, that you're driving down an interstate thinking you're headed toward one destination, and after driving for several hours, you realize something is wrong. You've been headed in the opposite direction. But instead of turning around, you just keep on driving because, after all, you mean to be going somewhere, and driving is at least getting you *somewhere*. Eventually, you've gone so far in the wrong direction that it seems impossible to get where you want to go. There's almost no point in even trying. That's what David did in the story we just went through.

But as you're driving, what do you see every few miles along the way? Exit ramps. David had lots of them. First, David found out that the woman was married. He didn't take that exit; instead, he accelerated right past it. A little while later, he found himself way off track, but he still didn't turn around. He could have owned up to his sin and perhaps even dealt with it quietly between Uriah, Bathsheba, and himself. That would have been embarrassing among a small group of people and may have created painful conflict between him and Uriah, but it wouldn't have necessarily cost anyone his life. On and on, David continued down the wrong road, just like we tend to do when we don't want to accept the consequences of what we've done. Maybe if we just keep going, the consequences will get less severe. But that's like continuing to drive in the wrong direction on an interstate. It only gets you farther away from your goal, not closer.

Step into the Story

Let me give you a word of advice. Go ahead and take the exit God provides, no matter how painful it is. He always provides one, and the next one isn't going to be any easier than this one. Restoration cannot begin until you get off the wrong road and start heading in the right direction.

Better than taking an exit is staying in the right lane all along. This situation would never have happened if David had done what kings normally do. Verse 1 tells us that David stayed home at the time when kings usually went out to war. So he wasn't where he was supposed to be on that night when he saw Bathsheba on the rooftop. Just as David could have avoided this whole crisis if he had been where he was supposed to be, we can avoid a lot of heartache for ourselves and our families if we keep ourselves on track. Staying in the right lane means guarding our hearts, which is getting harder and harder to do. We have temptations sent straight into our houses through the things that are on TV and that are accessible online.

If you're serious about having a heart after God's own heart, you'll risk someone else knowing the truth of what goes on inside of you. When you drag that secret out into the light, it loses its power to take you down the wrong road. The earlier these choices are made, the easier they are to make. But it's never too late to make them. Whatever you need to do to guard your heart and avoid a pattern of self-deception, it's worth it. And whenever God alerts you to the fact that you're headed down the wrong road, take the next exit ramp that brings you back into a place of integrity. Small, seemingly insignificant choices like that can have huge implications for your future direction. And there is always abundant grace and mercy for those who step out of deception and into the light.

↗ Questions for Discussion and Reflection ↙ .

• How much of your decision-making process is spent considering the long-term consequences? Why does our desire for immediate gratification often create a dangerous situation?

• Scripture speaks of a progression from desire to temptation to sin to death (James 1:14–15). How have you seen this progression play out in your life or the life of someone you know?

• Do you agree with the idea that sin is rarely a private matter because it has ripple effects in the lives of others? Why or why not? Whose lives were impacted by David's sin?

• In what ways do we tend to justify sin in our thoughts before we ever act it out? How can we prevent that dynamic?

• Why does sin tend to retain its power when it remains hidden and lose its power when it is brought into the light? Who do you know who is safe to talk to about personal issues? If you need to speak confidentially with someone, what steps can you take this week to make that happen?

CHAPTER 6

Arrogance vs. Humility— David and Nathan

2 Samuel 12

When a colleague and I went to Houston recently for a conference, we got there just in time for 108-degree weather and about 90 percent humidity. I'm thankful that they have great air conditioning in Texas, but when we were outside, walking across an asphalt parking lot and feeling the heat radiating back up at us, he and I just looked at each other in disbelief. I realize people there and in other parts of the country deal with that all the time, but for us it was intense. It felt oppressive and relentless. We could just feel our energy being sapped away.

That's the word picture David uses to describe what it's like to keep sin secret. It's oppressive, relentless, suffocating.

> When I kept silent, my bones wasted away through my groaning all day long. For day and night

your hand was heavy upon me; my strength was sapped as in the heat of summer. (Ps. 32:3–4)

I can say by God's grace that I've never committed adultery like David did, but there have been times in my life when I've hidden a secret. It's a burdensome feeling. What used to be fun isn't fun anymore. Work becomes heavy and draining rather than joyful and fulfilling. The joy of the Christian experience seems to vanish. That's how David described his experience, and I think most of us can relate to it. When we're living a lie, we become a strange, heavy mixture of guilt, embarrassment, fear, hypocrisy, exhaustion, apathy, and more. A life of secrecy is a hard burden to carry.

> When we're living a lie, we become a strange, heavy mixture of guilt, embarrassment, fear, hypocrisy, exhaustion, apathy, and more.

As the Bible wraps up the story of David's sin with Bathsheba, it describes how David resolved the situation. But it leaves the story awkwardly unresolved with a brief but ominous statement at the end of 2 Samuel 11:27—"But the thing David had done displeased the LORD." So God is displeased and David is miserable.

As we turn from chapter 11 to chapter 12, the background music has shifted to a minor key. There's a connection between God's displeasure and our misery. It isn't that He lays misery upon us as a punishment for our sin. That's just the natural consequence of stepping out of sync with His character and the way He made the universe to work. Like a fish out of water or a bird in a cage, we're missing our purpose if we're out of sorts with Him. He still loves us and calls us His children, but He doesn't rearrange His world to make our lives comfortable with our sin. So David is miserable, and he will remain that way until he deals with his sin the way God has ordained: by confessing it, turning from it, and experiencing His forgiveness.

There's a battle underneath the surface that involves more than just confession and repentance, not just in David's heart but also in ours. The crucible moment in this story pits arrogance against humility. Earlier, David's adultery and his cover-up demonstrate a willful disregard of God's law, as though the king after God's own heart was above the standards imposed on normal people. He abused his authority, a sure sign that a leader has some issues with arrogance. He placed his own interests far above the interests of everyone else, especially those of the man he set up to be killed. We don't see David's cautious respect for God's ways that he demonstrated earlier. We see a man who, at least temporarily, thinks much too highly of himself. Somehow, he has to regain the humility he once had.

God Pursues His Man

In the last chapter, we talked about how sending is an expression of authority. The person who sends—a message, a messenger, a representative, or whatever—is usually the person who has the higher status. Going, therefore, is an expression of obedience.

Now God steps back into the scene, not because David is seeking Him but because He is seeking David. It's His turn to send. That's how chapter 12 opens—"The LORD sent Nathan to David." In the last chapter, David was doing all the sending. He had marginalized God and was acting as though he was the lord of his own life. He sent someone to find out who Bathsheba was, sent messengers to bring Bathsheba to him, sent for Uriah at the front lines, sent Uriah to his home, and on and on. David was large and in charge. But though David may be king, God is the King of kings. Now He reasserts His authority.

We don't see the struggle that must have gone on in Nathan's mind. This could be a dangerous mission. If it were a classified ad, it would read, "Help wanted: confront the most powerful man in the nation. Compensation: possibly death. Retirement: out of this world. Serious applicants only." But we don't get any hints of wavering from Nathan. All it says is, "Nathan went."

But Nathan didn't go in with an accusation. He went with a story:

> "There were two men in a certain town, one rich and the other poor. The rich man had a very large number of sheep and cattle, but the poor man had nothing except one little ewe lamb he had bought. He raised it, and it grew up with him and his children. It shared his food, drank from his cup and even slept in his arms. It was like a daughter to him.
> "Now a traveler came to the rich man, but the rich man refrained from taking one of his own sheep

or cattle to prepare a meal for the traveler who had come to him. Instead, he took the ewe lamb that belonged to the poor man and prepared it for the one who had come to him." (2 Sam. 12:1–4)

God knows the way into our hearts. If Nathan had taken the direct approach, David probably would have been defensive and counterattacked. But David was a shepherd at heart, and Nathan came to him with a story that would surely resonate with David's experience. David loved sheep. Injustice in the context of shepherding would paint a very clear picture for him.

I've heard this passage presented as some kind of bedtime story to soothe David's nerves, but that's not what's going on at all. This is a legal case. It would not be unusual at all for the king to hear a complaint like this and render a legally binding decision to settle it. When justice was not served at a lower level and the parties had exhausted the appeals process, in some cases they could get a hearing with the king, who functioned as the "supreme court" of the nation. Usually the case would be presented for them by somebody already in the king's court—someone like Nathan. As far as David knew, Nathan's story was an actual case that needed to be settled.

> God knows the way into our hearts.

So Nathan explains that there were two men in a town, one rich and the other poor, and the poor man had only one sheep that he had carefully raised and nurtured and loved. "It was like a daughter to him."

I remember our family dog when I was growing up—Heidi. None of us kids were allowed in the living room. It had lime green shag carpet that actually came with a rake when we bought it. That was cool then, and Mom had to have it. I wear size 16 shoes, so my footprint was easily noticeable even then. Mom didn't need CSI to tell her when I had entered the holy of holies. We got to go in there Christmas morning and when we had company, with firm instructions not to break anything. None of these rules applied when grandkids came along, but those rules were sacred back then.

Heidi would come right up to the edge of the carpet and put her nose from the dining room into the living room. She would gradually claim more and more ground, just a little at a time, kind of like a first baseman stretching to catch the ball while keeping his foot on the base. Heidi mastered the stretch. And when I came home from my first year of college for Thanksgiving, Heidi had achieved full status where I had rarely been allowed to go. The dog had practically been granted a position in the family tree.

That's how pet owners feel about their pets, and that's how Nathan portrays the poor man's love for his lamb. This isn't just a farm animal; it's a beloved pet.

Then a traveler comes to the rich man. In Middle Eastern culture, hospitality is a highly valued virtue. Saying no to a traveler isn't an option. (David would have understood this well, having once been outraged when a man named Nabal refused to offer him hospitality.) Even today, it can be embarrassing how well you are treated when you visit Middle Eastern homes. They set before you extravagant feasts that sometimes cost a significant portion of a monthly salary. So the rich man in this story is culturally obligated as a host to provide for his guest. But in his selfishness, he passes by his own abundant flocks and takes the only lamb owned by the poor man to serve at his feast.

The Verdict Revealed, then the Crime

David was furious. He burned with anger and declared the verdict swiftly. "As surely as the LORD lives, the man who did this deserves to die! He must pay for that lamb four times over, because he did such a thing and had no pity" (2 Sam. 12:5–6). He not only issues the verdict, he's ready to move on to the sentencing. This crime is such an egregious offense that the defendant really deserves the death penalty. But the law doesn't allow the death penalty for lamb-stealing, so David imposes the maximum sentence he can: fourfold restitution.

What's interesting about David's reaction is that he has a remarkable ability to recognize the sin in someone else but is blind to it in himself. He isn't unique in that; we all do it. When other people's pride rubs us the wrong way, it's often because we have a good portion of it ourselves. I've seen drivers on the highway angrily honk their horns at the person who illegally cut in front of them without signaling—even while they themselves are illegally cruising at about twenty-five miles per hour over the speed limit.

I'm pretty good at this too. I couldn't ask for better kids, but I do it with them all the time. My daughter, Emily, is very intelligent and has a brilliant sense of humor, but sometimes the humor comes with an edge. She makes a convincing point, but at someone else's expense. And while I'm noticing that tendency so easily and urging her not to do it, the Spirit whispers to me something about how the acorn really hasn't fallen very far from the tree. And I hear my son, Philip, talk about his school work—how midterms are coming up, and three papers are almost due, and he's under so much pressure . . . yet he went hunting the weekend before, and he just got back from hanging out with his girlfriend's family for a couple of days. Everything in me wants to say, "Why are you procrastinating if you've got so much to do?" And again, the Spirit says, "Have you forgotten how you used to live in college, My friend?" And I'm pretty sure He's laughing when He says it.

David sees sin in this unnamed offender, and it makes his blood boil. He has spent months—maybe longer, but the text doesn't specify how long—deceiving other people, and when we do that, we become pretty good at deceiving ourselves too. So David is easily able to recognize the sin of the rich man but is completely blind to the sin of the man in the mirror. He declares guilt and announces the verdict, never realizing that he himself is the defendant.

That's when Nathan turns the tables. He reveals that David isn't the judge in this case, he's the defendant. He's the guilty, offensive rich man who so blatantly and callously stole a poor man's only treasure—and in this case, it wasn't just a lamb. It was a man's wife.

Nathan tells David, "You are the man!" (2 Sam. 12:7–10). Remember, this is a dangerous mission for Nathan. God told him to go confront the most powerful man in the kingdom and expose his sin. But Nathan doesn't pull any punches. He contrasts all of God's blessings with David's betrayal. God had given David the kingdom and wives, and He would have given even more if David had asked. But David did what was evil. Nathan charges David with the crime and, delivering a message from God, accuses him not only of despising God's Word but despising God Himself.

I don't remember what grade of Sunday school I was in when this story came up, but I can still picture the quarterly curriculum and its portrayal of this scene on a two-page spread. The artist had drawn Nathan with a skinny arm and the boniest hand on earth. The prophet's extremely long index finger was pointed directly at David, and the caption underneath said, "Thou art the man!" It was very dramatic, and actually kind of frightening. I wonder what David must have felt like when Nathan affirmed, "Yes, that verdict is correct, and you were the one on trial." The man after God's own heart was convicted of hating God and His Word. That had to sting.

Nathan doesn't stop with the verdict. Just as David had done a few verses earlier, Nathan goes straight into the sentencing phase of the trial. The sword will never depart from David's family. Calamity will come out of his own household. Someone close to him will sleep with his wives in broad daylight—an open reminder of what David has done in private. The *shalom* David had once enjoyed will turn to turmoil.

I don't know what I would have been thinking at this moment if I were David, but most kings would not respond well to such harsh words from one of their subjects. This is the crucible moment in the story. How will David react? The David portrayed before the time of Bathsheba would respond with a heart for God's truth. The David portrayed since Bathsheba is a bit more unpredictable and irrational.

Will David finally see the situation as God sees it? Will he understand what a terrible thing he has done? Or will he get defensive and lash out at the messenger? Will he remain in his self-deception—and his arrogance—and try to move past the whole sordid affair without ever really dealing with it? Will he banish Nathan from the palace and eliminate this threat to his authority?

The Turnaround

We aren't left to wonder about the answers to these questions for long. David responds to Nathan's charges with blunt honesty. "I have sinned against the LORD!" (v. 13).

It takes a lot of humility to own up to one's mistakes, especially those as big as the ones David has committed. The old David is back. For the most part, his life has been characterized by humility. He has been honest and upright, and he has respected those around him, even when they didn't deserve it. But in this most recent season of his life, he has been arrogant, abusive, callous, and seemingly unaware of the gravity of his actions. That's a hard state to break out of, and only something as pointed and jarring as Nathan's confrontation can do it. But when there's a confrontation like that, the response can go one of two ways—a softening of the heart, or a further hardening of it. David chooses the humble response.

It isn't easy to admit our mistakes. If you're traveling the wrong way down the highway and realize how far off course you are, you have to humble yourself to turn around—especially if you're a guy. I don't have a great sense of direction, and I remember lamenting that fact when Ellen and I were first married. I don't think her father had ever been lost in his whole life, so I'm sure it was a shock to her to be married to a man who will guess wrong about 75 percent of the time at a T intersection. Ellen would often look at me and ask, "Are you sure this is the right way?" And I'd answer, "Yeah, just trust me, baby." But I've learned over the years. Now she'll ask, "Which way feels like the right way?" And if I think, "Left," then she'll just smile, and I'll know to turn right. Yeah, that's humbling. But humility gets you where you need to be.

Nathan follows up David's confession with one more statement about the consequences. We might expect him to say something like, "That's okay. Now that you've recognized your sin and turned from it, everything will be fine." But that's not what God instructs Nathan to say. Instead, he informs David that God has indeed taken away his sin—David won't die for it. But because David's actions have caused God's enemies to show contempt for Him, the son that had been born to Bathsheba would die.

This is another reminder that sin always affects innocent victims. And I have to admit, this bothers me a little. Actually, a lot. It's one of those passages that causes people who don't follow the Lord to say, "If that's your God, I'm not interested." I wish I had a satisfying answer to explain God's decision, but I don't. And I don't think we're supposed to be satisfied about it anyway. This *should* be deeply troubling. Part of the Christian life is living with tensions like this and not having answers to the question, "How could God do that?" Even John the Baptist had to deal with that question as he sat in prison (Matt. 11:3). He sent messengers to Jesus asking, "So are You really the Messiah, or aren't You?" It wasn't clear because

131

Jesus wasn't doing what John thought a Messiah ought to do. He wasn't even freeing His friend and cousin from a Roman prison. The question that John had to deal with—and that every one of us has to grapple with—is, "Can we serve and follow a God that we don't fully understand?" The answer had better be yes, because if we can fully understand Him, He isn't a very big God. Sometimes we just have to say, "I don't know."

All I can say is that this is yet further evidence that sin has terrible repercussions and affects innocent victims. Our culture insists that whatever two consenting adults do is their own business and doesn't harm anyone else, but that simply isn't true. Sin creates ripples that impact others, whether we want it to or not.

> Sin creates ripples that impact others, whether we want it to or not.

This is also a severe reminder that confession doesn't remove all the consequences of our sin. You can probably think of times when your very sincere repentance didn't wipe away all the effects of what you had done. It restores your fellowship with God, which is a beautiful thing, but it doesn't remove all earthly repercussions.

When my son, Philip, was young, he and his Little League teammates would warm up by playing "soft toss" into the fence. Someone would toss the ball to the batter, who could then hit pitch after pitch straight into the fence and get lots of practice reps in a short period of time. The goal is to make sure your swing is level and your weight is properly distributed—developing muscle memory for the mechanics of the swing itself. Philip and his friend Garrison were doing that and had kept gradually inching away from the fence. Before they realized where their momentum was taking them, they had strayed a little too far back. Garrison tossed a ball to Philip, who got a good swing on the ball but hit under it too much. The ball soared high over the fence and toward the parking lot.

The lot was empty except for two vehicles: mine, and Garrison's family's brand new minivan. They had just bought it that week. It wouldn't have mattered much if the ball had hit my car, but instead it landed right in the middle of the hood of the minivan. And Garrison's mom was sitting in it. The boys stopped and stared. She didn't move. They waited and waited. There was no response. So they tentatively went back to playing soft-toss—this time a lot closer to the fence, where they should have been.

After several minutes, Garrison's mother got out of her car and walked with purpose in her gait toward the boys. The boys stopped playing for a second, and Philip said, "Oh, sorry, Mrs. Smith." And through clenched teeth, she answered, "Philip, 'sorry' doesn't cut it."

That phrase has become part of our family lore. Whenever any of us is a little too flippant with an apology, that's the response.

To his credit, Philip was very troubled and played a terrible game that day. Afterward he tried to make up for it. He went up to Garrison's mom and said, "Mrs. Smith, I'm so sorry. I apologize. That was terrible what I did. My dad will buy you a brand new minivan." That raises a different set of issues. Teach your kids what my seminary professor used to say: "You can't impart what you don't possess." But at least Philip had a desire to erase the consequences of his mistake. There just wasn't anything he could do about it.

That's often the dilemma after turning from the wrong direction and setting yourself on the right course. I've seen people who were thousands of dollars over their heads in credit card debt go through financial courses that helped them establish some spending boundaries and a debt and savings plan. They cut up their credit cards and say, "I haven't felt this free in years!" But then the next week, they come to church and look like they have the weight of the world on their shoulders. And if you ask them what's wrong, they seem shocked that the creditors keep calling and asking for their money. For some reason, the credit card companies don't seem to care that they repented.

That's because the guilt of sin and the consequences for sin are two different issues. I've known men who say, "I apologized to my wife for the affair. I came clean over a year ago. And she's still reluctant to be intimate. Pastor, you need to preach on unforgiveness." And my response is, "Really?" Repentance is good, but it can take years to rebuild trust. That's a consequence. Confession doesn't erase it. And if we don't understand that, we may begin to question God or our faith or the whole process of confession and repentance and forgiveness. That leads to some pretty unhealthy results. It's vital to remember that forgiveness wipes the slate clean with God, and it does reverse our course. But getting to the destination can still take time, especially if we've strayed far or for very long.

Life After Confession

Psalm 32, the psalm we looked at earlier that described David's burden when he was silent about his sin, is really a celebration about being forgiven. We can sense David's joy as he begins: "Blessed is he whose transgressions are forgiven, whose sins are covered. Blessed is the man whose sin the LORD does not count against him and in whose spirit is no deceit" (Ps. 32:1–2). He is relieved and free. The need to cover up is over. The deception is done. That word *blessed* can really be translated "happy," much like the beatitudes in the New Testament. David had come clean with God, and it felt good.

The story could end there, and back in Sunday school, it did. But there's an epilogue that encourages us with God's ability to redeem and restore. Second Samuel 12:24–25 tells us that David and Bathsheba have a son and name him Solomon. God loves this son and sends word to give him a second name: Jedidiah—"loved by God."

Who does God send to bless the child? Nathan the prophet. He's still around. If I had been the king, I would have followed up that last encounter with a brief "thank you" to Nathan and a parting gift of a one-way ticket to a distant province. I don't think I would want him around anymore, even if I had agreed with his pointed verdict against me. Bathsheba and David knew the truth, but the only other person to know might have been Nathan. Would he talk? That's a risk. And it would have been easy to justify sending him away for the sake of the nation and to put that whole difficult season in the past.

But God blesses David and Bathsheba with a son named Solomon—whose name, by the way, comes from the word *shalom*. David's peace has been restored. And David continues to demonstrate his humility by keeping Nathan in the court. He still listens to him. I believe Nathan turns out to be David's closest friend, his most trusted adviser. He has already proven that he's a good friend by doing one of the hardest things a friend has to do: speak the truth in love.

I think that's the ultimate expression of friendship—to risk rejection and speak the truth in love. A lot of people won't tell the truth to their friends because doing so would jeopardize the friendship. In my experience, people tend to be truth-tellers or lovers. Few people combine those two attributes very well. In the first church I pastored, I knew a lady who certainly knew how to speak the truth. She told me she had the gift of confrontation. I don't remember that being in any New Testament list of spiritual gifts, but I agreed that she had it. On the other side are people who are so focused on love that they don't want to hurt any feelings or strain any relationships. I tend to be out of balance in that direction, but Scripture keeps pulling us back to the middle. Speaking the truth in love is a unique blend, and Nathan seems to have mastered it. That's a sign of a good friend.

In his rediscovered humility, David recognized Nathan's friendship for the treasure that it was. There's a passage in 1 Chronicles that confirms this. It's hardly noticeable at first; it's one of those genealogies that usually causes us to zone out until we get to the next story.

David reigned in Jerusalem thirty-three years, and
these were the children born to him there: Shammua,
Shobab, Nathan and Solomon. These four were by
Bathsheba daughter of Ammiel. (1 Chron. 3:4–5)

Did you notice anything unusual about those names?
These are the children born to David and Bathsheba, and
the third one listed is named Nathan. Stop and think about
that for a minute. If there was any time in David's life that he
would like to forget, it was surely those painful few months
when he had committed adultery, had an innocent man killed,
and then had to be confronted by a prophet of God in order to
snap out of his delusion. The whole thing was shameful and
embarrassing. And now David and Bathsheba are preserving
the memory of it in the name of one of their sons? This little
Nathan would be a daily reminder of the pain. Every time
they were called to dinner, the name "Nathan" would ring out.
No stuffing the memory, no secret past, no shying away from
the man who called the king on the carpet. David embraced
his past because there was something of value in it for him.

This is one of the greatest expressions of humility I can
find in David's life. The ultimate celebration of friendship is
to name your own child after your friend. My brother's name
is Steven Roger Tuttle. Why Roger? Because in World War
II, another soldier from Iowa like my dad, who slugged it out
across France and into Germany with him but never made
it back home, was named Roger. That's a tribute to a good
friend, and apparently that's the kind of relationship David
had with the man who announced God's harsh discipline to
him. David and Nathan had a bond, and David celebrated that

bond by naming a child after Nathan—even though that bond was forged from David's most painful memories.

A Lasting Legacy

A few Christmases ago, I was reading the genealogies of Jesus. I have to admit I don't hang out there very often. I know all Scripture is profitable for us, but I stumble through the names like everyone else, and it's hard to get enthusiastic about who begat whom. But as I was reading the genealogy in Luke 3, something jumped out at me. In verse 31, it mentions "Nathan, the son of David." (That's how I first discovered David had a son named Nathan; I spend even less time in 1 Chronicles than I do in the genealogies of Matthew and Luke.) And I realized that not only had David honored his friendship with Nathan by naming a son after him, but God had also honored this son by giving him a place in the genealogy of Jesus.

Do you realize what that means? It means that God took a family line that was never supposed to happen and redeemed it so thoroughly that it became part of the Messiah's lineage. The Luke genealogy traces Joseph's lineage one way (specifying that Joseph was only "thought" to be the father of Jesus, but His actual father was God Himself), and Matthew's genealogy traces the lineage another way, through Solomon. Jesus therefore descended from a marriage that began through David's sin.

I don't know how that makes you feel, but I'm encouraged by the fact that God takes all of the flaws of the human race, somehow accounts for them ahead of time, and still works out His plan through them. Mark Bailey, president of Dallas Seminary and a board member for Walk Thru the Bible, preached a message based on the genealogies a few Christmases ago. He began with, "Hi, I'm Jesus, and I'm from a highly dysfunctional family." On the human side, the Messiah's family tree is filled with some pretty unusual nuts. That's not an isolated theme in Scripture; read about the patriarchs. Their families were infected with all kinds of infighting, rivalries, marital dysfunction, violence, and everything else that puts the "fun" in dysfunction. When the Bible tells us we have a high priest who can relate to our struggles, it's true. Every family has its quirks and oddballs—and even its secrets. Ellen is still meeting some of my uncles who were too risky to introduce to her back when we got engaged. That's how human families are.

God works through the mess anyway. David and Bathsheba, who came to be a couple through illegitimate means, ended up having two children who became part of the Messiah's genealogy. That speaks volumes about God's ability to redeem our worst mistakes.

> God takes all of the flaws of the human race . . . and still works out His plan through them.

But there's even more to the legacy of David's humility than a couple of names in the sacred lineage. David wrote one of his best-known psalms in the immediate aftermath of his confession. Psalm 51 beautifully captures his grief and repentance. It pleads with God to create a pure heart in David, to renew his spirit, to maintain the presence of the Spirit in David's life, and to restore the joy of his salvation. Then verse 13 declares what David would like to see happen in the aftermath of this whole affair: "Then I will teach transgressors your ways, and sinners will turn back to you."

Isn't it just like God to use the recorded words of David to answer his own prayer? After David asks for his joy to be restored and for his heart to be steadfast and for the opportunity to tell others about God's ways, isn't it just like God to say, "Okay, let's include your prayer in My Word so it will cross cultures and centuries and show people what to do with their sin"? There wasn't even a temple where sacrifices were made for sin in David's time, but eventually a Messiah would come, not only to cover sin like a sacrifice but to remove it forever. And God would connect the dots of history through a descendant named after the most painful time in David's life. Only our God does things like that.

David wanted his mistakes to be a learning opportunity for others, and his desire was granted. We continue to be moved by his words of repentance today. Millions throughout history have learned from them and been inspired by them. Millions more have been warned by David's example of the dangers of self-deception and sin. God so thoroughly redeemed the awkward, painful, crisis moments of David's life that they have impacted generation after generation of lives.

Step into the Story

Maybe your life is one of those that is impacted by David's experiences. Perhaps you're even living with a secret right now and need to bring it into the light and experience God's *shalom,* the healing and wholeness of His redemption. There have been times in my life when I've been humbled to the point of not even knowing what to say to God. In those moments I've turned to Psalm 51, and sometimes all I can do is read it out loud and let it be my voice. The Holy Spirit somehow communicates the message in a way I don't even understand.

Let this story from David's life cultivate your own humility as it shows us his. Sometimes you might be the Nathan in this story, speaking the truth in love to a friend who needs a heavy dose of reality. But sometimes you're the one in need of a Nathan. You're off course, joyless, hiding a secret, weighed down by a burden you can't carry anymore. If that's true, pray Psalm 51 to God, turning over each request in your mind and letting it settle into your heart. With all humility, ask the Lord to give you a clean heart and restore the joy of your salvation. Let Him renew your spirit and cover you in His presence. And experience the freedom of a heart in full fellowship with God.

↗ Questions for Discussion and Reflection ↙

• How do you think David felt after his cover-up appeared to be successful? Do you think he was content? How do you feel when you're spiritually not in sync with God or when you're trying to keep a secret?

- How do you think Nathan felt when God sent him to David with a difficult message? Is obedience to God always safe? Why or why not?

- How do you think the David who had so much integrity earlier in his life transformed into a king who acted like he was above the law? In what ways have you seen success impact people negatively?

- Do you think we can ever avoid the consequences of our sin? In what ways does God's forgiveness cover our sin? Why does forgiveness for sin not erase the consequences of it?

- Do you think it's true that "whatever happens between two consenting adults is no one else's business"? Why or why not?

- What can we learn from Nathan about the importance of speaking the truth in love to others? Why do you think David did not reject Nathan for confronting him?

- In what ways did God redeem David's sin? What does that tell us about how He deals with our past mistakes?

CHAPTER 7

Entitlement vs. Sacrifice— David and Araunah

2 Samuel 24

America's Keswick conference center in New Jersey holds retreats and training sessions and conferences, just as its name suggests. But it also oversees the Colony of Mercy, a Christ-centered recovery ministry for men who are addicted to alcohol and drugs. For more than a hundred years, the Colony of Mercy has been changing the lives of men through God's Word and fellowship with each other.

I speak almost every year at the conference center, and I get to see the fruits of its ministry. The men from the Colony of Mercy often serve meals and do the maintenance for the conferences as part of their residential requirements. And in each session of a conference, at least one gives his testimony. I've heard story after story of changed lives, sometimes even from wives who can't believe the change they see in their husbands. I realize no addictions recovery center has a 100 percent success rate, but this one is significantly more successful than others because it teaches men to draw their life from Jesus. Seeing relationships restored and personal Goliaths defeated is heart-warming and encouraging.

As president of a global ministry, I often speak at certain events simply because they are strategically important for the ministry and its relationships. But that's not the main reason I speak at Keswick. I speak there because it's good for me. The first time Ellen and I went there, we didn't come with the best attitude because of our overloaded schedule. And unlike many of the conference centers where we've stayed, America's Keswick is a no-frills kind of place: relatively Spartan conditions, no TV, not the softest mattresses, and pretty much the polar opposite of speaking on that cruise around the ports of Italy. So when we arrived, already not in a great frame of mind, it felt like a chore to be there—until Ellen picked up a brochure and began reading about the history of the place and its Colony of Mercy. She realized it was the same ministry that had started a program in North Carolina, where years before, her grandfather finally met Christ and found freedom from his alcohol addiction after several failed rehab attempts. We both suddenly realized that this conference center was part of her family story.

We felt spiritually slammed, almost like we were standing on holy ground. We suddenly got a different perspective. This was what ministry and life-change are all about. This is where people come face-to-face with their brokenness—a condition we all share but rarely admit—and find an eternal solution for it. To listen to story after story of how God met people in their time of need was a cleansing experience for us. And every time I go, I experience the same thing. I'm so glad I have an opportunity to be there.

Underneath much of our discontentment in life is an attitude of entitlement. We expect things to be a certain way or to work out as we wanted, either because we've paid our dues and deserve certain rewards or because we assume that God or life implicitly promised us a pleasant and comfortable existence. That's where our hearts go sometimes, and it often takes a very humbling experience to break us out of that place.

The opposite of entitlement is a spirit of sacrifice, not in the sense that our lives have to be hard and painful, but in the sense that life's greatest gifts are meant to be shared with others rather than hoarded for ourselves. I believe God frequently gives us the opportunity to switch gears—to move from a mind-set of taking in to a mind-set of pouring out. That's what being at Keswick and seeing its Colony of Mercy does for me; it puts me in a position of having to acknowledge my true priorities. Our tendency is to gravitate toward entitlement, but God uses experiences like this to pull us back into a spirit of sacrifice. He restores in us the joy of serving.

That's an important perspective for a generation steeped in self-centeredness. All generations of human history have been pretty self-focused—that's part of our fallen condition—but we seem to be living in a particularly unashamed culture of entitlement right now. Our society is known as one of the most litigious in history because we somehow got the impression that we should be compensated for every slight offense we ever suffer. College students today often expect professors to give them good grades, not because they've earned them but because their tuition is paying the professors' salaries. Often when people "give" money to a cause or to a church, invisible strings are attached, as though the gift entitles the giver to a measure of control over the recipient.

This attitude carries over into ministry too. I've known people, usually from other cultures, who are shocked that I don't fly first-class or come with a large entourage to speak at events. That's what they have come to expect from the president of a ministry: first-class tickets and lots of helpers, along with a substantial honorarium and accommodations in a four-star hotel, all of which seem to function as status symbols. In some cultures, pastors expect to have a driver provided for them once their church gets to a certain size. When Walk Thru the Bible began working in one particular Asian country, one of my colleagues, John, met with conference organizers and local pastors to go over the logistics and schedule of the training event. One of the organizers assured John that he and the other visitors from the U.S. would be served expensive food in a separate dining room from the pastors attending the conference. That was their way of demonstrating appreciation and showing hospitality, but it also conveyed a message that some people were more entitled to special treatment than others. Neither John nor anyone else from Walk Thru the Bible would expect anything other than fellowshipping with our hosts during meals. When John insisted that the Americans would eat "common food" together with the local pastors—that it's not really church if there are separate tables—the organizers were a little surprised. But word got out to all the attendees that the Americans wanted to eat with them, and it created enormous good will for the duration of the conference. At least a dozen people thanked John for joining them at mealtime.

Don't get me wrong. The hospitality extended to me, to others who work in ministry as a profession, or to any other leader in any field is a blessing. There's nothing wrong with enjoying generous gifts. But there's a difference between enjoying and expecting, and it's amazing how easily those perks evolve into subtle expectations. Before long, we "serve" in a spirit of entitlement and contribute to a culture of elitism. Blessings become expectations, which then become requirements. We feel that if we've "paid our dues" or achieved a particular status, life should be handing us its rewards.

Meanwhile, Scripture tells us to put on humility and serve one another. It emphasizes sacrifice. So some of our crucible moments will shine a spotlight on any attitude that conflicts with our humility and service. They will put us in a position of having to choose between feeling entitled and giving sacrificially.

Several episodes in the life of David reveal a sacrificial heart. One of the most jarring aspects of the story of David and Bathsheba is that it revealed the opposite: a heart that was seeking its own momentary satisfaction rather than pouring itself out for others. David operated out of a sense of entitlement throughout that season of his life. But that was the exception, not the pattern. God gave him plenty of other opportunities to express his true values and priorities and to demonstrate a sacrificial spirit, and David made the most of those opportunities.

Give What Is Costly

Near the end of his reign, David took a census of Israel and Judah against the advice of his general and, as it turns out, of his own conscience. Scripture doesn't tell us why the census was wrong—God Himself had ordered censuses in the past—but apparently David's focus was on the human strength of his kingdom rather than on depending on God. When David realized his sin and repented, God gave him three options for how to be disciplined. David chose perhaps the most immediately painful but also the shortest in duration. A plague fell on Israel, seventy thousand people died, and in His mercy, God stopped the plague as it approached Jerusalem. When David saw the angel of death, it was standing by the threshing floor of Araunah the Jebusite. So David, in response to the words of a prophet, decided to build an altar to God on that site.

David went to ask Araunah about buying the land so he could build an altar, but Araunah offered it to him freely. He was more than willing to honor the king and God by giving not only the land but also animals for the first sacrifice. Maybe he was so grateful that the plague stopped at his land that he was in a generous mood, or perhaps he was such a loyal subject that he couldn't imagine charging the king a selling price. Regardless, the site was available to David for the taking. All he had to do was say yes.

David could have taken the land for the good of the nation—an "eminent domain" rationale for the benefit of all in his kingdom. Some kings wouldn't hesitate. Years later, the wicked queen Jezebel would press her husband, Ahab, to seize a vineyard from its owner because she felt that the king ought to have a royal right to take whatever he wants. But David wouldn't embrace such an offensive sense of entitlement. After all, it was his sin that caused the plague, not the nation's. This was personal. So David refused Araunah's offer and insisted on buying the land.

What was David's rationale? "I will not sacrifice to the LORD my God burnt offerings that cost me nothing" (2 Sam. 24:24). In this crucible moment, David paid fifty pieces of silver for something that was offered to him freely, built an altar there, made his sacrifice to God, and received an answer to his prayer. The plague on Israel was formally ended.

Think about David's statement and what it means for us today. Our offerings should cost us something. I know a lot of people who give sacrificially to God's work, but the statistics about how much Christians give as a percentage of income are frighteningly low. The majority of church attendees put an amount in the offering plate that can hardly be called a "sacrifice." Most people, me included, usually aren't forfeiting a nice vacation or new furniture when they give. In our culture of giving today, the general trend is to skim off the top in a way that doesn't put a dent in our lifestyle. We lump it in with other "disposable income." Some have more disposable income than others, so they are able to give larger amounts. But they aren't necessarily giving larger sacrifices. We have a tendency to give to the Lord that which doesn't cost us quite enough to hurt.

Jesus pointed this out when He observed a widow making her offering at the temple. A lot of people had come by and put in large amounts; the loud clank of their heavy coins could be heard in these very public receptacles. But a widow came by and put in two mites—tiny coins that were hardly worth anything. Jesus commended her for offering more than all the others. Why? Because He was looking at what it cost her. The offering was big not because of the size of the sum but because of the size of the sacrifice.

David was aware that for his offering to be a true gift to God, it should cost him something. There should be a sacrifice involved. He may have been entitled to the land, but that wasn't the issue. In the kingdom of God, sacrifices are expressions of love. A cheap gift can be given from a casual heart, but a costly gift almost always comes from devotion. We see that in the expensive perfumed oil a woman poured on Jesus' feet, we see it in the persecution of the early church, and we see it in the martyred ministers and missionaries who have given their lives in service to God.

And we especially see it in Jesus, who emphasized that He came not to be served but to serve (Matt. 20:28), who washed His disciples' feet and told them to serve each other in the same spirit (John 13:1–17), and who emptied Himself of all the privileges of deity, took the form of a servant, and offered His own life (Phil. 2:5–11). Jesus was entitled to remain in heaven enjoying all of its pleasures and ruling His realm. But He chose to enter a hostile world. Why? Because something important was at stake, and it could only be accomplished through sacrifice. That's what the Son of God chose. An attitude of service and sacrifice is part of His very nature and central to His kingdom. Entitlement is not a kingdom virtue. Pouring one's life out for God and others is.

We can't do that unless we have an attitude of humility. The problem is that deep down inside, most of us cling to the remains of a *quid pro quo* relationship with God. When we serve Him, we subconsciously expect Him to reciprocate. We don't mean to; that's just how human nature works. We find that most people operate that way, and it's really hard to get that mind-set out of our system when we start relating to God. And while it's true that we have entered into a covenant relationship with Him in which we can expect Him to fulfill the promises He has made, this covenant is based entirely on grace. Even our expectations about God have to be rooted in humility because we didn't deserve them. This is not a tit-for-tat relationship. We receive from God everything and more through identifying with His Son, but by nature, we aren't entitled to any of it.

One of Walk Thru the Bible's instructors and a close friend, Gerald Robison, has a creative way of looking at this. He and Bob Sjogren call it "cat and dog theology." They contrast the attitudes dogs and cats have and use them as parallels for how we relate to God. If you were a cat, you might be highly offended by the analogy, but if you're a cat owner you would probably agree. Dogs say, "You pet me, you feed me, you shelter me, you love me . . . *you must be God!*" Cats, on the other hand, receive the identical treatment and say, "You pet me, you feed me, you shelter me, you love me . . . *I must be God!*" Christians who think like cats read the

> Deep down inside, most of us cling to the remains of a *quid pro quo* relationship with God.

Bible and conclude that the story is all about us. Christians who think like dogs read the Bible and conclude that the story is all about God. And though Bob and Gerald would readily acknowledge that most Christians know how to talk like dog theologians, those words rarely translate into a God-oriented lifestyle. We live more like cat theologians—or "me-ologians." The dog attitude is focused on the master, while the cat attitude is focused on what the master can do for him.

Jesus told a short parable that is aimed at undermining an attitude of entitlement in the people who serve Him. He described how ludicrous it would be for a servant to come in from the field and be invited by the master to eat his fill first. The master doesn't thank the servant for doing what he was hired to do. The servant takes care of all the master's needs first, *then* takes care of his own. This is a surprising parable in that Jesus, our Master, spoke often of how He came to serve. Clearly He wasn't focused on imposing His authority on unwilling subjects. He was apparently instilling a sense of servanthood in His followers. He actually encouraged them to say, "We are unworthy servants; we have only done our duty" (Luke 17:10). There's no entitlement in that. Only humility.

Relinquish Rightful Claims

Much earlier in David's life, we get a glimpse of his wrestling with a sense of entitlement. Before he was king, while he was on the run from Saul in the desert, David and his men appealed to a nearby wealthy landowner for some help. The man's name was Nabal—it literally means "fool" or "disgrace"—and he lived up to the meaning. He was callous and self-centered, and he refused hospitality to these travelers.

As we discussed earlier, hospitality is a prominent virtue in Middle Eastern culture, both then and now. It's assumed. Especially in ancient times, to refuse hospitality to a traveler was tantamount to putting the traveler's life at risk. There was no nearby grocery store. The gas station down the road didn't have 32-ounce fountain drinks. The desert could be extremely unforgiving toward those who didn't bring enough supplies into it or took too long to cross it. So when someone making a living in the land encountered someone who was passing through, the host had a certain moral obligation to meet the visitor's needs.

But Nabal rejected David's request. He sent David's messengers back to him, basically saying, "I don't know who you guys are or what master you're avoiding, but I'm not wasting my goods on you." And David was furious.

David had every right to expect hospitality from Nabal. He had treated Nabal's shepherds well in the past—his later explanation indicates that he had actually protected Nabal's property from thieves—and he was entitled to some kindness in return. For a moment, David let that sense of entitlement fuel his anger. He and about four hundred of his men armed themselves to go up against Nabal and his servants. He was fully prepared to take revenge.

Nabal's wife Abigail intervened. She was beautiful and sensitive and understood the foolishness of her husband. She gathered supplies and sent her servants ahead to meet David and his men on the road. And then she followed without telling her husband where she was going. When she got there, she bowed down, absorbed the blame for her husband's foolishness, pleaded with David not to have blood on his hands, expressed her confidence that God would do as He promised and make David king, and asked David to remember her in the future.

David was moved, even though moments earlier he had sworn to slay every one of Nabal's men by morning. He relented, and Abigail went home. Within two weeks, Nabal was dead, and David did indeed remember Abigail. He married her. On the verge of reacting out of entitlement, he was spared from a horrible mistake by her wisdom. He was able to set his entitlement aside and embrace the humility she demonstrated.

This story doesn't exactly highlight David's sacrificial spirit. He was ready to go to war and had to be persuaded not to. But it does shed light on how we behave when we feel entitled—even when we *rightfully* feel entitled. It reminds us of a very important principle: that simply having a right does not require us to defend or enforce that right. Just because we are granted certain rights and privileges doesn't mean that we have to zealously demand every benefit of those rights and privileges. Sometimes it's better to forfeit a right than to engage in conflict over it. God loves justice, but He doesn't love it when we demand it for ourselves. He wants us to live with humility.

This is a common theme in Scripture. Jesus told His followers to turn the other cheek, not even things up. He urged them to go the extra mile, not meet the minimum requirement—even for an unreasonable demand. Paul told the Corinthians it would be better to be defrauded than to create conflict with other Christians in court. As we saw earlier, Jesus Himself demonstrated the ultimate relinquishing of rights when He left behind the privileges of deity in order to come to us in human flesh, live as a servant on our behalf, and give up His life for us (Phil. 2:5–11). He told His followers not to take the seat of honor at a feast but to take the lowest-status seat instead (Luke 14:7–11). Nowhere in Scripture are we told to get all we can or to make sure no one ever steps on our toes. That doesn't mean we are required to submit ourselves to abusive situations, but we have to be careful about our motives and attitudes. Are we genuinely in need of protection or provision? Or are we trying to get even or just offended that someone didn't recognize our rights? A sense of entitlement, whether legitimate or false, will often provoke us to actions that aren't helpful for relationships. God is always drawing us away from that attitude and encouraging us to live with humility and a sense of sacrifice.

Here's why: God is purely relational, and His kingdom is based on relational values. Sacrifices—acts of service toward Him and others—are relationship collateral. When we offer Him or others something that is costly to us in terms of time, effort, or resources, it makes a statement about how much we value that relationship. A humble attitude goes a long way toward building fellowship and bonding with others. But a sense of entitlement runs in the opposite direction. It isn't relational at all; it's self-focused. Instead of bringing people into our lives, it draws boundaries for how they should treat us. Entitlement doesn't cultivate relationships; it limits them. Sacrifice and service, on the other hand, are an investment in the needs and desires of those around us. They are expressions of love.

Does that mean we should have no boundaries in our relationships? Of course not. We live in a world full of dysfunctional interactions, and it's appropriate to make sure we are treated respectfully as we try to do the same for others. Boundaries aren't wrong. But when the attitude behind them is entitlement— "I've got to maximize my rights and get all I can get," though we would hardly express it that way—we've adopted a perspective that isn't consistent with God's character.

> Sacrifice and service are an investment in the needs and desires of those around us. They are expressions of love.

David crossed that line for a moment and then by God's grace and Abigail's gentleness was pulled back into a more generous frame of mind. We need to become sensitive to that line in our own lives so we can be aware of the times we're crossing it. God may provide an Abigail to rein us in, but ideally we'll develop enough of a sacrificial spirit to live from that attitude all the time. It's always good in a crucible moment for humility to rise to the top.

Offer What Is Precious

After 2 Samuel 23 records "the last words of David," a summary of his "mighty men" gives us a brief but insightful glimpse of his sacrificial spirit rising to the top. It's in a flashback to the days of exile, when David and his men were hiding out in the cave of Adullam in the wilderness. A Philistine detachment had taken over Bethlehem, David's hometown. One day, David remarked to his men that he longed for the water he used to drink from a certain well there. "The Three"—an elite threesome who stood out among the thirty mighty men who were closest to David—took it upon themselves to satisfy their leader's longing, and they broke through Philistine lines and brought some of that well's water back to David. The significance of this act was not lost on David; he realized they had risked their lives to quench his thirst with his favorite water. What would have been just a tasty drink suddenly became a precious treasure to him. And whatever was a precious treasure to David was destined to become a precious gift to God. This water was as sacred as the blood of his men. David couldn't drink it. Instead, he poured it out as an offering.

Modern readers are often shocked by David's wastefulness. "These men risked their lives to get that water for him, and he won't even honor them by drinking it? If he's just going to pour it out on the ground, they might as well have not gotten it in the first place!" But that's not how David saw it. All throughout Scripture, God calls us to give Him offerings from the first and best of our harvests. Whether that's money or grain or whatever we produce from our resources, that goes to Him. He is worthy of our best. When David saw what his men had done for him, that water's value skyrocketed. And whatever is highly valued in the eyes of a servant of God makes a worthwhile offering to Him.

Was David entitled to that water? Of course he was. His men obtained it specifically for him. But here's where we see a clear difference between entitlement and sacrifice. A spirit of entitlement says, "Whatever is of high value is worth keeping." A spirit of sacrifice says, "Whatever is of high value is worth giving." If the current of our lives is flowing inward, we'll focus on the value of what we're getting. But if the current of our lives is flowing outward, we'll focus on the value of what we can offer.

> A spirit of entitlement says, "Whatever is of high value is worth keeping." A spirit of sacrifice says, "Whatever is of high value is worth giving."

We naturally have our "flow switch" turned to "incoming." We're out to get, gather, acquire, and achieve. It takes a profound spiritual transformation for that switch to flip so that we more naturally think in terms of giving. That doesn't mean we can't ever receive anything. It's impossible to give what we don't have. We need a constant inflow from God and His resources in order to have anything to offer. But is our focus on getting in order to keep, or in getting in order to give? Scripture always emphasizes a sacrificial lifestyle toward God and others—giving, offering, and dedicating whatever we have. That doesn't mean we can't enjoy His good gifts; many godly people have been blessed with guilt-free abundance. But they aren't watching over their blessings to make sure they don't lose any of them. Whatever we receive from God, our default attitude should always be relational.

A person after God's own heart is extravagantly generous because God Himself is extravagantly generous. A heart full of Him *wants* to give.

Years ago when our kids were young, our church was collecting coats for a Christmas service project for those in need. Because the children in the church felt that "even poor kids don't want clothes for Christmas," they decided to collect toys instead. Emily was only five or six at the time, and her grandparents had given her a hard-to-find Cabbage Patch doll the previous Christmas. She loved that doll; it had quickly become her favorite. She didn't even allow her friends to play with it when they came over. But that's what she chose to contribute to the collection. Never mind that she had a "pet net" full of stuffed animals that she never played with and wouldn't have missed. Or that her grandparents were coming to town for Christmas in a couple of weeks and would love to see her playing with the doll they had given her. That's the doll she wanted to give.

Like any rational parents, Ellen and I tried to talk her out of it. We were thrilled that she embraced the spirit of giving, of course, but this was a little over the top. "I'm sure they would enjoy another stuffed animal. You have plenty. Maybe you could give two or three of the stuffed animals from your 'pet net' that you never play with. I'm sure they would love to find a good home." We were sure she would miss that doll and later regret that she had given it away, and we also wanted her grandparents to see her playing with it. But we were also sending a mixed message, teaching our kids to be generous and then trying to temper their generosity.

Emily seemed to pick up on that and got pretty upset. I'll never forget what she said: "Why are you stopping me from doing a good thing? When God wanted to love us, He didn't send us some extra kid from His pet net. He sent His only 'bregotten' Son." Her pronunciation might not have been perfect, but her theology was better than mine.

Young children have a way of reminding you of your own values sometimes. Emily insisted on giving the doll because that was the point—to give something valuable. We were undermining the very lessons we had been trying to instill in her. God loves a sacrificial spirit, but we often try to minimize it so it isn't quite so costly. But isn't that the nature of a sacrifice? It *has* to be costly. That's exactly what God modeled for us in giving us the life of His Son. And that's exactly how He calls us to live toward Him and toward others.

Step into the Story

Jesus told His followers that if they spent their lives trying to gain what they could—if their "flow switch" was always set on "incoming"—they would lose the kind of life they were looking for. But if they lost their lives for His sake—if they flipped that switch to "outgoing"—they would find the life they wanted. They would receive the life they had just sacrificed. In other words, living from a sense of entitlement quenches life, and living from a sense of sacrifice makes it flourish. That shouldn't be a difficult choice; as Jim Elliot's most famous quote puts it, "He is no fool who gives what he cannot keep to gain that which he cannot lose." Those who abandon the relentless and elusive quest to get, gather, acquire, and achieve actually receive far more than they could ever want.

There's a word that was much more commonly used in the past to describe a certain character trait than it is used now: *magnanimous*. It means "very generous or forgiving," especially in situations where you don't have to be. It's an open-hearted demeanor that gives people a lot of latitude for their quirks, flaws, mistakes, and perceptions. That's the kind of character welcomed in the kingdom of God. It fits His nature. It's the kind of attitude that goes ahead and lets a pushy person into the lane in front of you on the highway because, after all, that second and a half that you might save by holding your place in line might not be worth the stress involved for either of you. Or that prompts you to go out of the way to serve someone just because it feels good to serve. Or that says, "This time I'm going to donate my time and energy instead of donating the leftovers I didn't want anyway." Or that causes you to sympathize with a cranky person having a bad day rather than snap back at him. In short, it's a refusal to live from a sense of entitlement and a choice to make sacrifices, large and small, wherever they are needed. And most of all, it's a desire to pour your life out to God because it's the highest and best you can offer.

↗ **Questions for Discussion and Reflection** ↙

• What evidence do you see of "entitlement" in today's world? What evidence do you see of people living sacrificially?

• What do costly gifts, whether to a person or to God, demonstrate about our values and feelings? Do you think a willingness to sacrifice for someone is always evidence of love? Why or why not?

• Why is it important to give up rightful claims in our relationships with others? Read Matthew 5:38–42. Why do you think Jesus taught these principles? How do you think people would respond to us if we lived out these truths faithfully?

• Why do you think David poured out the water that his men had risked their lives to get for him? How do you think they felt about his offering? How do you think God felt about it? Why?

• What does your level of generosity say about your values? Are there any adjustments you need to make in order to live more sacrificially? If so, what?

CHAPTER 8

Disappointment vs. Expectancy— David and Solomon

1 Chronicles 28–29

Ellen and I longed to have a family after I completed seminary, and we planned to have our first child nine months after graduation. I shared some of that experience in chapter 5, but what I didn't mention was how long the frustration lasted—many months and then years of disappointment over failed attempts, while our friends' families continued to grow. We began to doubt and question. *Surely this was what God wanted. Surely He was the One who had placed these desires in our hearts.* Years after we were married and several surgeries later, Emily was born. Then after three more years of struggles, Philip came along. We got two precious children, but we lost a third and wanted more. Our plan and timing had been different from God's. During those long years of yearning, we learned to wait and trust . . . to accept . . . to hope . . . but never with a guarantee of reward. At times our dream seemed to be more of a burden than a blessing. We looked forward to something we only hoped would be fulfilled.

In a fallen world, yearning is a universal human experience. We want to accomplish something significant. We want to have an impact that lasts longer than our lifetimes. Sometimes we just want to be fulfilled. These yearnings can be expressed in a number of ways: the desire to be married, to have children, to fulfill our career dreams, to be physically healthy, to see all of our loved ones come to Christ, to be financially stable and comfortable, and many more. And they can be threatened by broken relationships, illnesses and injuries, rejection and betrayal, bankruptcy and foreclosures, and death. We live in the tension between desire and fulfillment, and sometimes that tension leads to the very acute pain of disappointment. Every human being experiences it at some point. But not everyone responds in a way that honors God and ultimately brings fulfillment to themselves.

You have a desire. Quite a few of them. Some of them come and go easily, but you probably have several that have become rooted deep in your heart. Sometimes your desires are fulfilled, sometimes you hold on to them in expectation, and, if you're like most people, some of them have been set aside because it doesn't look like they will ever be fulfilled. Navigating our dreams and desires can be a tricky adventure, especially when we're walking with a God for whom nothing is impossible. This God can accomplish anything, but He also has specific plans and purposes for us. Discovering how those plans and purposes line up with the dreams in our hearts is a process.

David had an intense desire. Scripture is very open about it—both in his own writings and the histories written about him. Somehow, even though God had never given instructions or expressed a desire for a permanent temple, David wanted to build one for Him. He dreamed of a place where people from his own country and beyond could come and meet with God. He yearned to experience God's presence and to make that experience available to others. He wanted God's worship center to be a permanent structure in an established capital city.

Long before, God had given Moses the design for a tabernacle—a mobile worship center where priests could offer sacrifices and people could gather to experience God's presence. It was a temple for nomads, the place where the ark of the covenant and the articles for worship would be housed. But that was in the wilderness, and centuries after His people had entered the Promised Land, the worship center was still a tent. It had been located at Shiloh and at Gibeon at various times since the people had entered the land, but its location was still theoretically temporary, even after more than three centuries. And God had never suggested otherwise.

When David established the kingdom's capital as Jerusalem—a conquered Canaanite city formerly known as Jebus—he brought the ark there and put it in a tent pitched especially for that purpose. He assigned priests and musicians the responsibility of establishing a ministry of praise and worship around the ark, but the tabernacle itself remained in Gibeon. That's where the altar was and where sacrificial offerings were made. But David's deep desire was to unite the two worship centers in a permanent building in his capital.

This was more than just a political maneuver or a king's wish for a legacy. It was a profound passion. It shows up in several of David's psalms, in which he writes of the temple as though it were a current reality. Psalm 27:4 is one of the best-known examples: "One thing I ask of the LORD, this is what I seek: that I may dwell in the house of the LORD all the days of my life, to gaze upon the beauty of the LORD and to seek him *in his temple*" (emphasis added). We often read this simply as an expression of love for God's dwelling place, forgetting that the temple had not been built in David's lifetime. It would be a future promise for the next generation, not a present possibility. We don't know when this psalm was written—whether it was before or after God told David when the temple would be built—but we do know it expressed an unfulfilled longing at the time it was written. David wanted to encounter God in God's own house.

But God said no. Actually, that's not exactly true; He didn't specifically deny David's request. He deferred it. He said yes, but not now and not in the way David had hoped. For whatever reason, the man after God's own heart, who treasured a godly desire to honor God's name by establishing a place of worship, was not given the fulfillment of his desire. Sometimes God says no even to people who have a heart like His.

The crucible moment in David's life that we want to look at in this chapter isn't in the desire he had or the answer God gave him. It's in David's response afterward. Everyone experiences disappointments, but they don't make or break our lives. The way we respond to them, however, has a lot to do with our fruitfulness and joy. We can be paralyzed by them, withdrawing into apathy or even bitterness; or we can press through the pain, adjust our vision, and be drawn into a higher purpose than we dreamed. David's choice in that crucible moment impacted God's kingdom for generations to come.

> Everyone experiences disappointments, but they don't make or break our lives.

David's Great Request

Soon after David brought the ark to Jerusalem, but long before his sin with Bathsheba, he hinted at his desire to Nathan the prophet. "Here I am, living in a palace of cedar, while the ark of God remains in a tent" (2 Sam. 7:2). David recognized how his lifestyle misrepresented his true priorities. He was living in luxury while the holy place of God's special presence was being relegated to the kind of shelter used by desert wanderers. It didn't make sense.

We have moments like that. We marvel that our society pays star athletes millions of dollars to play a game while ministers, teachers, nurses, soldiers, and many other self-sacrificing hard-working people labor for extremely long hours in order to just scrape by. Something seems inherently wrong with that picture: those who can entertain us for a moment are rewarded financially far more than those who can impact future generations with their character and service. Every culture has such inconsistencies, sometimes valuing what doesn't have eternal or lasting significance over what does. David's recognition of this inconsistency in Israel is much like our awareness that Christians spend far more on personal lifestyle enhancements than on missions, or that seemingly frivolous industries in our culture are thriving while churches and ministries are barely making payroll. At some point, it hit David that Israel's holiest site was temporarily housed behind fabric walls while he was living in a grand palace of expensive materials. And he knew that wasn't—or shouldn't be—an accurate reflection of his or his nation's values.

So David mentioned this conundrum to Nathan, and Nathan didn't even ask what David wanted to do about it. He knew that however David wanted to correct the situation, it came from a right perspective and a godly desire. David was looking back on years of God's faithfulness and recognized that God had delivered him from danger and put him in a position of influence. He was grateful for all God had given him and wanted to do something great for God in return. How could any counselor or adviser deny the nobility of such a request? Nathan couldn't. If anyone could be trusted to come up with a God-honoring plan in this situation, David could. "Whatever you have in mind," Nathan replied, "go ahead and do it, for the LORD is with you" (2 Sam. 7:3).

These are the words of a prophet who has a track record of hearing from God. In later stories, Nathan's words to David will be a remarkably accurate expression of God's heart. But here, his prophetic declaration gives blanket approval for David to carry out his desire. Is Nathan making too many assumptions with his approval of David's yet-unknown plan? Does he think he knows God's specific desires well enough to represent them without asking about them? Is this situation so obvious that no prophetic insight is necessary? Whatever the case, Nathan gives approval first and listens to God later. And he is undoubtedly surprised when God comes to him that night with a different answer.

God's Surprising Answer

In the next few verses, God instructs Nathan to give David a message. His message begins with a series of questions: "Are you the one, David? Have I ever asked for a permanent building? Have I ever suggested that I need more than a tent?" Then God reminds David of Israel's history: "I've moved with My people wherever they have gone with only a tent as My dwelling. I've never dwelt in a house." And then He reminds David of his own history: "I took you, a mere shepherd, out of the fields to be ruler of My people. I've been with you through everything. I've delivered you from your enemies." All of this—the questions and the history—seem to be setting David up for a big "no." But that's not exactly what God says.

God doesn't tell David, "Yes, you can build Me a temple," but He does give David some really extravagant promises. He says He will make David's name great, like the greatest men on earth (v. 9); He will plant Israel firmly in the land where they can be free from oppression (v. 10); He will give David rest from all his enemies (v. 11); He will establish the kingdom under one of David's sons (v. 12); that son will build the temple (v. 13); and David's lineage and kingdom and throne will endure forever (v. 16).

On the surface, this is less than what David asked for; David will not be able to build something great for God. On the other hand, the answer is greater than the request. David's vision was for a building project and a worship center; God's promise is for a great name and a throne that lasts forever. David wanted to honor God, yet God deflects it and chooses to honor David instead. It isn't the answer David and Nathan expected, or that we would expect either. But it was an answer—and a good one.

Most of us can relate to this dynamic in our relationship with God. The normal pattern is for God to answer specifically what we ask of Him, but sometimes we ask for one thing, and He gives us something else. When that happens, we may console ourselves with the thought that His answer is better than what we asked for, but deep down we may be tempted to lament the loss of our hope. We receive something good from God, but our original desire remains unfulfilled.

We get glimpses of this dynamic in the ministry of Jesus too. Once when He was preaching in a home in Capernaum, some men lowered a paralyzed friend down to Him through the roof because they couldn't get close enough to Him through the doorway. Clearly they had one thing in mind: they wanted Jesus to heal their friend. That was their desire. That was the implicit request. So how did Jesus answer? He addressed a different need. He forgave the man's sins.

Were these men disappointed in the answer or excited about it? It wasn't exactly what they asked or expected, but it was, in the eternal scheme of things, much greater than what they had asked for. But somewhere deep inside, they had to have been disappointed. They wanted to see their friend walk, and Jesus' first answer to them wasn't a yes.

Jesus didn't let that disappointment linger long. He soon healed the man after using the occasion to prove a point to the religious critics around Him. In fact, the healing demonstrated that Jesus had the authority to forgive sins in the first place. But that moment between an unexpected answer and the fulfillment of a hope—a very long moment in some of our lives—can be a bitter letdown.

How would you feel if you had been in David's place? On the one hand, God affirmed David's desire. He essentially said yes to the temple, even while saying no to David. So which was David's greater desire—that the temple be built, or that he be the one to build it? David could have gotten hung up on the fact that he wasn't the one, just like many of us have a hard time on our missed opportunities that others get to fulfill. When we deeply desire to make a difference in God's kingdom, and then have to watch someone else fulfilling our desire, it isn't easy to swallow. I've known people who have an intense desire but no apparent opportunity to serve in a certain country or pursue a particular career or to raise children. It's painful to watch them as they see other people doing the exact things that were on their hearts to do. Should they rejoice that the spiritual needs of the country they wanted to go to are being met, even though not by them? Or that God is raising up people to pursue that significant career and accomplish great things for His kingdom? Or that a generation of godly children are being brought up by the friends and fellow church members around them? Maybe, but that's a lot to ask.

When we have what seems to be a God-given desire burning within us, we want to be the ones to fulfill that desire. When God opens that opportunity to someone else, it hurts.

David could have been offended that God gave the assignment to the next generation. He could have nursed that pain for the rest of his life. We'll see how he doesn't do that, but for now, even in God's answer, we can see a grace that David couldn't possibly recognize yet. The son who will build the temple would be Solomon—one of the sons from David's relationship with Bathsheba, which began in adultery and technically should never have happened. Apparently, long before that sin was committed, God anticipated the fruit of it. He knew Solomon would be among the offspring and already had a great assignment for him. At the time, before the story was finished, God's answer could have been offensive to David; in retrospect, it was full of grace that David didn't even know was needed yet.

When we get disappointing answers from God—or delayed answers or silence—many of us easily slip into a "why me" attitude and stay there for a while. The God who can easily accomplish anything with just a word, who sits on His throne in heaven and does whatever He pleases (Ps. 115:3), has apparently chosen not to fulfill the desire of our heart in the way or the timing we hoped for. That's hard to get over, especially when we can't see the end of the story. Being offended or hurt is a profound temptation.

David's Surprising Response

When Nathan reported God's answer to David, Scripture shows us none of those tempting negative responses. In fact, David responds very positively, at least on the surface. "Who am I?" he asks, realizing that he doesn't deserve God's favor and His promises but can receive them freely as gifts. Over the next few verses, he worships God for His goodness. He doesn't ask why, he doesn't argue with God (although on other occasions in his psalms and elsewhere, he isn't shy about his questions), and he doesn't sink into self-pity. He pours forth praise.

David also asks God to do as He promised—a request that might seem superfluous to us but is common in Scripture. If God promised, won't He accomplish it without being asked again? Perhaps, but biblical prayer often reminds God of what He has said and lays hold of it by faith. David recognizes God's promise and takes it to heart. He affirms God's trustworthiness and asks for God's continued blessing.

David could have focused on his disappointment but didn't. There can only be two reasons for that: (1) he wasn't all that disappointed because the temple wasn't a big deal to him; or (2) his own vision for his life was less important to him than God's vision for his life. We know from other evidence in the Bible that David continued to dream about the temple—we saw that in Psalm 27:4 and will look at other examples later—so this wasn't an easy desire to dismiss. The reason he was able to refocus must have been that he trusted God's vision for his life. So he worshipped.

Think about those areas of your life where you have experienced the denial or delay of your dream. Is it in finding the right person to marry? Waiting to be healed from a physical problem? Praying for a loved one to come into a relationship with Christ? Or is it a dream that was on its way to being fulfilled yet was lost or broken along the way, like a divorce, a bankruptcy, or the death of a loved one? Whatever

> We have to look beyond the disappointment and choose to believe what we cannot see with our eyes.

the case, if your heart is filled with a burning desire, and that desire is deferred, worship is not a natural reaction. In order to praise God in our disappointment, we have to make a choice not to see His goodness through the lens of our circumstances but to see our circumstances through the lens of His goodness. We have to look beyond the disappointment and choose to believe, at least for the moment, what we cannot see with our eyes.

This is a battle we will face all of our lives. When the serpent slithered into Eden, his words to Eve questioned God's goodness. The temptation was an attack on God's intentions toward His people. Why would He create fruit that looked good to eat, place it in the middle of the garden, and then say not to eat it? Or, to put it in more modern terms, why would God give us hearts that have strong desires—often very good and godly ones—and then not fulfill those desires? From the beginning of human history, these are questions that linger in the back of our minds, and we have a choice to make. Will we trust that His heart is good, whether or not our circumstances make His goodness obvious at any given moment? Or will we grow skeptical of His intentions and let disappointment color our perceptions forever?

David made his choice and demonstrated it by worshipping God as soon as he learned that his deep desire would not be fulfilled in his lifetime. He put all of his focus on what God did allow him to do rather than on what God didn't allow him to do. In this crucible moment, he chose to trust God's hidden ways and adjust his vision. He didn't deny his desire or try to quench it; he simply redirected it to fall in line with God's will.

Desire Redirected

This is an important aspect of this story that many people miss. David never said, "My desire isn't important. It didn't matter anyway. God isn't interested in my dreams." That would have been an overreaction to God's decision and a denial of how God works in our lives. He very often cultivates dreams in our hearts that He wants us to pursue. We should never value those dreams more than we value Him, but we don't need to deny that they are important. And David didn't. It's as if he said, "Okay, Lord, if that's what You want, I'll pursue that passion in Your timing and support Your plan for carrying it out." Somehow he was able to adjust his vision to line up with God's.

How do we know David held on to his dream of building the temple? Near the end of his life, he demonstrated that he had been taking positive steps toward the temple project, even though he would not be able to accomplish it in his own time. God's answer to him hadn't quenched his desire; it had simply changed his focus.

David knows his life is nearing its end when he summons all of his leaders and officials to assemble in Jerusalem. When they all arrive, he stands in front of them and begins perhaps his last public address:

> "Listen to me, my brothers and my people. I had it in my heart to build a house as a place of rest for the ark of the covenant of the LORD, for the footstool of our God, and I made plans to build it. But God said to me, 'You are not to build a house for my Name, because you are a warrior and have shed blood.'" (1 Chron. 28:2–3)

He then goes on to describe how God had taken him from being a shepherd to being a king, chosen his son Solomon to succeed him and to build the temple, and promised to establish his kingdom forever. He charges Solomon to follow God's commands and serve Him wholeheartedly—and to do the work David was forbidden to do. He urges his son to build the temple as God had said.

What happens next is very revealing. David gives Solomon the plans for the temple—detailed plans for every building and room (1 Chron. 28:11–18). David had not been sitting around lamenting the loss of his dream. He had blueprints for the dream to be accomplished. The text says these plans were put into David's mind by the Spirit. In other words, though God said no to building the temple in David's lifetime, He said yes to daydreaming about it, cultivating a vision for it, developing details and logistics, and taking steps toward the fulfillment. David not only gave instructions for the building, he had also envisioned how the priests and Levites would serve, how they would divide their responsibilities, and how the articles of worship would be made—down to the specific weight and material of each fork and dish. David considered these specifics to have come from the hand of the Lord upon him. "He gave me understanding in all the details of the plan" (1 Chron. 28:19).

David encouraged Solomon to be strong and courageous, not to lose heart, and to know that God was with him. He gave him access to all the workers who could contribute their skills to the project. He provided the raw materials—precious metals, jewels, stone, and wood—out of the kingdom treasury and his own personal wealth. He collected gifts from the people who were willing to invest their resources in the project. And he offered a prayer of dedication committing the entire endeavor to God.

Clearly David didn't bury his disappointments and live a life of resignation. Many of us do; we subdue our hopes in order to protect ourselves from disappointment. But David didn't shy away from his deep desire, even though he knew he wouldn't live to see its fulfillment. Instead, he invested whatever he could in every aspect of the dream he could legitimately participate in.

We can learn a lot from that. We're allowed to pursue aspects of a dream even when we can't pursue the object itself. But we have to open our eyes to those possibilities. When God doesn't answer us as directly or specifically as we want Him to, we are sometimes so focused on the promise He *isn't* giving us that we miss the promise He *is* giving us.

David had received extravagant assurances from God, and he fully expected God to fulfill them. Instead of embracing dejection, he embraced his role in God's plan. And he adapted his desire to fit it.

> We're allowed to pursue aspects of a dream even when we can't pursue the object itself.

Not only did David do the things described in 1 Chronicles 28–29, we also see evidence of his passion seeping through some of his writings. Psalm 27:4 proclaims the "one thing" he desires: to dwell in the house of the Lord, gaze upon His beauty, and seek Him in His temple. The temple shows up in other psalms too. In fact, the superscription of Psalm 30 says it was written as a dedication for the temple. Do you realize what that means? Years before the first stone of the temple would ever be laid, David not only had all the blueprints and priestly assignments and weights and measures of the temple project, he also had written verses to be read at the dedication ceremony. He would make sure that even in his absence, his presence would be felt.

Look at that list of David's preparations again and let it sink in. David . . .

- charges the leaders (1 Chron. 28:8)
- charges Solomon (28:9–10)
- gives Solomon the plans (28:11–19)
- encourages Solomon (28:20–21)
- gives his royal and personal resources (29:1–5)
- collects gifts from the people (29:5–9)

- commits the whole project to God (29:10–20)
- writes a psalm to be read at the dedication (Ps. 30)
- lets himself long for something that isn't going to be completed in his lifetime (Ps. 27:4)

It's as if David did everything possible up to the point of building the temple without actually beginning construction. He celebrated the fact that God's plan is bigger and better than any single generation. He was able not only to lay the foundation for the next generation; he was also able to look into the next generation and rejoice in its accomplishments as though they were his own.

It has been said that if your dreams can be fulfilled in your lifetime, then your dreams were too small. That's a perspective few people have today, but it's a necessary attitude in God's kingdom. God has wired His creation in such a way that seeds sown in one generation often bear fruit years or even centuries later.

> God's plan is bigger and better than any single generation.

Hebrews speaks of many who looked ahead to God's promise without experiencing its fulfillment; they were commended for their faith even though future generations would receive the rewards of it (Heb. 11:39). Abraham was one man whose family grew into a nation, which grew into a kingdom, which grew into a global faith. Jesus spoke of the kingdom of heaven in terms of a small mustard seed that grows into a plant large enough for birds to come and nest in it. God is a master of taking small, seemingly insignificant, and apparently unlikely or unbecoming things and making something great of them—but rarely quickly. His work takes time and crosses generations. Anyone who wants to do something of significance in His kingdom will have to be content not seeing the end of it. The best we can do is lay a foundation and set up the next generation to add to it. We get to see some of the results of our labor along the way, but if it's really lasting, it will continue to produce results long after we're gone. That's how the kingdom works. David, the king whose throne would last forever, seemed to grasp that.

Step into the Story

What disappointment weighs heavy on your heart? What big regret stands out in your life? Most people can identify something immediately, but the real question is this: What would it look like for you to move beyond your disappointment and embrace your role in God's plan? That may not be easy to do—in fact, it may be the most difficult choice you've ever made—but you can still choose to do it. Like He did with David, God gives you an invitation into something greater, a bigger picture than you may have imagined for yourself. You have the option of embracing His purposes and stepping into something that will last well beyond your lifetime.

It's essential to maintain this big-picture perspective. No matter what God has said no to, He has said yes to something else. You may not have heard the details of that promise yet, but it has been in His mind since long before you were born. He has a destiny planned for you, and it's probably bigger than what you've dreamed of. If you can get past the disappointments in your life, choose to believe in His goodness regardless of what you see, and embrace whatever invitation He offers with whatever degree of passion you've been given, you will find yourself living with the same sense of purpose David had.

Just remember, however, that what looks like a "no" right now may not be one at all. David wanted to build a temple, and God didn't say no to that idea. In fact, He said yes, even though Scripture tells us He hadn't expressed a desire for a permanent temple. This was something on David's heart, and God agreed to it. He just didn't agree to let David be the one to fulfill it. Even so, He allowed David to participate significantly in the preparation. David's desires were important to Him.

God does not take your disappointments lightly. And much of what might look disappointing to you now isn't a "no" answer, it's a deferred answer. Maybe He has delayed in order to prepare you for the answer. The process we go through while we are waiting for Him to fulfill a promise is often the exact training we need to be able to bear the weight of the fulfillment. Sometimes He lets us endure long silences not to discourage us but to provoke our hunger and draw us deeper into relationship with Him. Whatever the reason, we often get discouraged in the middle of the story, long before He shows us how it's going to end. Just remember that every good story has tension and disappointments in the middle, and every good story has a satisfying, fulfilling ending. Like David, we need to refuse to get stuck in the middle of the story. One way or another, God will take responsibility for our desires, giving us satisfaction in their fulfillment or encouragement for the ones that are delayed or redirected.

We can take great comfort in one of the verses David penned: "Delight yourself in the LORD and he will give you the desires of your heart" (Ps. 37:4). Some people believe that means He satisfies whatever desires we have if we delight in Him. I think it means that He will plant the desires in our hearts that He wants us to have. But however we interpret the verse—whether God grants the desires we have or puts His desires in us in the first place—it assures us that when our greatest passion is God Himself, the desires of our hearts will line up with the things He has planned for us. There will be congruence between what God does *in* us and what He wants to do *through* us and *for* us.

> He will plant the desires in our hearts that He wants us to have.

Frederick Buechner said, "The place God calls you is where your deep gladness and the world's deep hunger meet." He wires His people with passions that can only be fulfilled when we are seeking His kingdom purposes. Ephesians 2:10 expresses it this way: "We are God's workmanship, created in Christ Jesus to do good works, which God prepared in advance for us to do." When we embrace His promises and purposes, He will lead us into a place of satisfaction—even if it takes some faith and time to get past our disappointments. When we make that choice and pursue Him above all, one way or another He will give us the desires of our hearts.

↗ Questions for Discussion and Reflection ↙

• Why do you think David was so zealous about building a temple? Do you have a vision of something you would like to do for God? If so, what is it?

• How do you think David expected God to answer his request? What is the difference between having expectations of God and having faith in Him?

• How do you think David felt after he heard God's answer? How do most people respond to God when they are disappointed? How did David respond?

• Have you ever tried to worship God in the midst of a disappointment? What are some of the thoughts we have when we're disappointed that can hinder our worship? In what ways does worship amid disappointment honor God?

• How did David reshape his dream to fit with God's plans? In what ways was he able to pursue his dream in spite of not fulfilling it?

CONCLUSION

David was far from perfect. At various times he was rash or dishonest, his loyalties toward others weren't always clear, and he wasn't a great model of parenting when his kids were in turmoil. He was a complex figure, and we don't want to oversimplify him.

But David was also very human, which makes him a great subject for those of us who want to know how to live with the same kind of passion and purpose. In spite of all his flaws, the testimony of Scripture is that he had a heart for God, his kingdom would be blessed forever, and he would serve as a foreshadow of the Messiah. It's hard to argue with those credentials. When God makes an example of someone, it's a pretty good idea to actually look to that person as an example.

That's what we've done in this book. David lived with passion and purpose, and God endorsed him as an example of having the right kind of heart. If we want to know what a person "after God's own heart" looks like, we can see that it involves having strong character, fearless faith, a commitment to do what's right, the humility to repent when we've done wrong, the resolve to keep going, a sacrificial spirit, and an expectancy and hope that God will accomplish His purposes. And if we want to know how to avoid a life of mediocrity, we can see that sloppy character, fear, opportunism, despair, cover-ups, pride, entitlement, and regrets are not our friends. These positive and negative traits aren't visible only in David's life; they show up throughout Scripture. But in critical situations—in the crucible moments that make or break the trajectory of a person's life—there's hardly a better person to emulate than the man whose heart God commended.

In our efforts to live with passion and purpose, we need to be aware of the crucible. The critical moments of our lives aren't obstacles to avoid or challenges to get through. They are the testing ground of our character and the molder of our hearts. God refines us in these moments, transforming us to be more like Him and strengthening us for greater things. This is where children of the King become the kingdom's finest citizens and demonstrate the nature God has put within us. These are not the moments that break us; they are the moments that launch us into places God has prepared for us. This is where God-like hearts are forged.

That's why, as uncomfortable as the crucible might sound, it's never something to avoid. If we want to do things like slay giants, learn God's timing, and work toward our God-given dreams, our journey will take us into the crucible from time to time. It's a necessary part of God's plan for us. When the heat turns up, our hearts are tried and tested and transformed. But all we have to do is look at the legacy of David to see that the crucible is worth it. What goes into it won't remain the same. But what comes out can last forever.

ABOUT WALK THRU THE BIBLE

For more than three decades, Walk Thru the Bible has been dedicated to igniting passion for God's Word worldwide through live events, devotional magazines, and resources designed for both small groups and individual use. Known for innovative methods and high-quality resources, we serve the whole body of Christ across denominational, cultural, and national lines.

Walk Thru the Bible communicates the truths of God's Word in a way that makes the Bible readily accessible to anyone. We are committed to developing user-friendly resources that are Bible centered, of excellent quality, life-changing for individuals, and catalytic for churches, ministries, and movements; and we are committed to maintaining our global reach through strategic partnerships while adhering to the highest levels of integrity in all that we do.

Walk Thru the Bible partners with the local church worldwide to fulfill its mission, helping people "walk thru" the Bible with greater clarity and understanding. Live events and small group curricula are taught in more than forty languages by more than thirty thousand instructors in more than one hundred countries, and more than one hundred million devotionals have been packaged into daily magazines, books, and other publications that reach over five million people each year.

Walk Thru the Bible
www.walkthru.org
1.800.361.6131

About Phil Tuttle

As president of Walk Thru the Bible, Phil travels the world teaching, equipping, and encouraging pastors and leaders to share God's Word with the unreached and under-served. Phil received his Bachelor of Arts in Christian Education and Bible from Wheaton College, and a Master of Theology in Christian Education from Dallas Theological Seminary. Phil and Ellen have been married more than thirty years and have two adult children, Emily and Philip.

About Chris Tiegreen

Chris Tiegreen has inspired thousands of people through *The One Year at His Feet Devotional, Story Thru the Bible, 90 Days Thru the Bible,* and his many other books. His experience as a missionary, pastor, journalist, and university instructor bring a unique perspective to his writing. Chris is currently a writer and editor at Walk Thru the Bible.